WAKE UP, IT'S A CRASH!

WAKE UP, IT'S A CRASH!

The Story of the First Jumbo Jet Disaster
A Survivor's Account

EARL MOORHOUSE

DAVID & CHARLES

Newton Abbot   London   North Pomfret (Vt)

British Library Cataloguing in Publication Data

Moorhouse, Earl
 Wake up, it's a crash!
 1. Survival (after airplane accidents, shipwrecks, etc).
 2. Aeronautics — Kenya — Nairobi — 1974
 I. Title
 916.76'25   TL553.9
 ISBN 0-7153-8093-1

Library of Congress Catalog Card Number 79-19214

First published in South Africa by Jonathan Ball Publishers

Printed in Great Britain
by A. Wheaton & Co. Ltd., Exeter
for David & Charles (Publishers) Limited
Brunel House Newton Abbot Devon

Contents

This book is for my sons, Garett Jon and Brendon Scott Moorhouse, and for all those who took flight LH540 out of Nairobi, Kenya, on November 20, 1974.

Introduction

ON MARCH 3, 1974 I was on my way to catch a plane from Johannesburg to Nairobi, Kenya, when I heard that a Turkish Airlines DC 10 had crashed shortly after takeoff from Orly Airport in Paris. Three hundred and forty-six people had been killed.

Traveling on the airport bus I listened to the other passengers nervously discussing the crash. It was the first disaster involving a wide-bodied DC 10 jet and, at that time, the greatest number of people killed in a single air accident. I remember a woman asking, "Do you think they knew they were going down?"

A man replied, "It was probably so quick they didn't know a thing."

"I wonder what they thought about – if they *did* know," the woman asked. No one in the bus replied and the question hung in my mind, worrying me all the way to Nairobi.

Nine months later I learned the answer myself when the Boeing 747 I, my wife, and our two sons were on crashed in the African bush outside Nairobi. Ironically, I was en route to take up a job that had been offered to me as a result of the trip I made to Nairobi on the day of the Paris crash.

Two years had to pass before I could attempt to write this book and even then I only started it at the insistence of relatives and friends when I realized that they and others shared my original curiosity about the thoughts and reactions of crashing air passengers. During those two years I had to answer basically the same queries over and over again; if those questions had not been asked this book would probably never have been written.

What does it feel like to know that the aircraft you are flying in is crashing, that in seconds your life might be over? What thoughts flash through your mind, and how do you react? There cannot be more than a few hundred people on earth who are able to answer these questions, and even fewer writers.

This book is an attempt to describe what we and our fellow passengers experienced when Flight LH540 crashed on the morning of November 20, 1974. It is not, it should be emphasized, an attempt to blame or criticize the West German airline, Lufthansa, which has an outstanding safety record. All airlines have crashes. Lufthansa was simply unfortunate in that it was operating the first Boeing 747 that crashed — an event the media had been expecting ever since the aircraft went into service six years before. In that time, 747s carried an estimated 73 million people without a fatal incident, a most remarkable safety record, almost without precedent in aviation history. Yet all that was forgotten the moment our jet went down in flames and the horrific story was splashed across the front pages of the world's newspapers and broadcast on radio and television.

This book is chiefly about people. Those seeking detailed technical explanations of what went wrong aboard the jumbo *Hessen* that fateful November morning will have to search elsewhere. The few technical details given are based on the official report of the East African Community Accident Investigation Branch, a copy of which was secured for me by the Community's Chief Inspector of Accidents, Mr. D.C. Stewart, in Nairobi. I was also fortunate in having the advice of Mr. Andrew Wilson, aviation writer for *The Observer* in London. His several articles on jumbo jet safety, published after the 1974 accident, and a number of telephone conversations helped to simplify some of the technical issues I encountered. Tracking down fellow survivors and witnesses on the ground was a major task. When I started work on the book I wrote to Lufthansa asking for their help and for particular items like the passenger and crew list, and a copy of their internal accident report. They replied:

It is, we regret to say, quite impossible for us to assist you in this project. Apart from our natural (and, we believe, understandable) hesitation to rejoice at the prospect of seeing a book published about the unfortunate events which took place at Nairobi, we face a number of more basic problems.

You asked for a complete list of passengers, including those who survived, and their addresses. Passenger lists are made available only to the public prosecutor or legal courts. We are also bound by law not to supply such information to third parties as this would constitute invasion of privacy. We hope you understand that we could become legally at risk if the persons concerned discovered that we had released their names and personal details. This could lead to court proceedings against our airline.

For the same reasons, we do not release personal information about our crew members. Here, too, we are, as employers, under obligation not to supply such names to third parties.

Lufthansa's accident report has turned into a fair-sized volume, and that, too, is strictly confidential because it is an internal company document, and to release it is out of [the] question.

Without Lufthansa's help, I had to discover the survivors' names and addresses the hard way. The obvious starting point would be those newspapers that had carried reports of the crash and listed the names of local survivors. With the help of my wife, Lynn, I sent off for copies of the major British, American, German, South African and Kenyan newspapers and soon received copies of their editions of November 20 and the day afterward. We spent the next few weeks cross-checking names in the various reports and eventually compiled a near-complete passenger list. But what about addresses?

We went through our newspapers a second time, noting nationalities and hometowns. In some reports survivors' occupations and businesses were mentioned; newspapers from Johannesburg featured interviews with survivors' relatives and friends who had been waiting for the flight at Jan Smuts Airport. All this information was noted down under the name of the survivor concerned.

Because we were living in England at that time, tracking down the British survivors was fairly easy. We simply looked up the names in the telephone book, narrowed the possibilities down to two or three entries and called them up.

Tracing the addresses of survivors in other countries was a little more difficult. I spent time at embassies in London checking their telephone directories, and wrote off to the most likely addresses. In some cases I wrote to embassies, newspapers and company offices requesting their assistance in contacting survivors whose names did not appear in telephone directories. Some survivors, like Margaret Hooker, were contacted through relatives. From a newspaper report I traced her brother, Mr. Jimmy Laing, in Johannesburg and learned that Margaret was living in a town close to London. I phoned her up and met her in a matter of days.

By a stroke of luck I was given the address of the Kahn family of Dallas, Texas, who were members of a Unitours party touring Africa. I wrote and asked if they might have swapped addresses with other members of their group and a week later, thanks to Renate Kahn, received all the names and addresses I needed.

In many cases, survivors helped my investigations by passing on the names and details of their friends or business associates who had been on the flight. My writer friends, Jock and Betty Leslie-Melville, and Dancy Bruce, who live in Nairobi, pursued various contacts and witnesses on my behalf. They also put me in touch with the Board of the Nairobi Hospital which very kindly drew up a special report of the hospital's activities on November 20, 1974, and gave details of the type of injuries the staff treated. Once traced, I had to interview the survivors, their families and friends, and the many witnesses on the ground. Some submitted themselves to personal interviews; others taped or wrote their experiences for me, or sent press and magazine clippings along with detailed explanations and descriptions. All endured my many follow-up questions without complaint. A few survivors declined to describe their experiences at all because they found the memory too painful. One survivor declined because, at the time of the accident, he was a non-paying guest of the airline.

Despite all efforts, there are still survivors who have not been traced. Only two days before I traveled from Johannesburg to London in June 1979 to work on this book I managed to contact yet another survivor, Manfred Wengerek, who lives in Bedfordview near Johannesburg. My wife and I spent several hours with him discussing the crash and the effects it had on us. We were the first fellow survivors he had met since 1974 and the discussion was obviously therapeutic for him. He discovered that we too had suffered from claustrophobia, bouts of depression, nightmares, and an inability to make decisions.

Several survivors reported that they felt better after sharing their experiences, and it is my hope that this book might help others who have had similar traumatic experiences and cast light on the way such events affect our lives.

Many people have helped to create this book and I am particularly grateful to the following: John and Jean Bing of Johannesburg; Dancy Bruce of Nairobi; Kay Cokayne of Pretoria; Mr. D. C. Stewart, Accident Investigation Branch, East African Community, Nairobi; Mother Dietlinde Geis of Eshowe, Zululand; Rudi Hahn of Deitzenbach; John Hall of Johannesburg; Colonel M. J. Harbage, Nairobi Hospital; Mr. J. L. Beecher, consultant surgeon, Nairobi Hospital; Tillie Harmel of Dallas; Hermann Hennecke of Johannesburg; Erich Hesse of Berlin; Gisela Hutton of Johannesburg; Bruce Hobson of

Nairobi; Margaret Hooker of Middlesex; Pat and Ian Horsfield of East Grinstead; Robert Horsfield of Johannesburg; Squire Horsfield of Cape Town; Gino Iannibelli of Taranto; Karl, Renate and Nancy Kahn of Dallas; Gerd Kampf-Emden of Essen; John Kingsley-Heath of Gillingham, Dorset; Bob Laburn of Johannesburg; Jimmy Laing of Johannesburg; Jock and Betty Leslie-Melville of Nairobi; Carol Mall of Sumter, South Carolina; Hans Neeb of Minden, West Germany; Joseph Odiyo Onguru of Nairobi; Peggy Ottenheimer of Baltimore; Jill and Terry Partridge of Eckington, England; Mr. J. Rillaerts, of Brussels; Tom Scott of Bad Soden, West Germany; Hans-Joachim Schacke of Bad Nauheim, West Germany; Edmund and Elinor Senkler of Seattle; Henriett Smith of Wedgefield, South Carolina; Malcolm Solts of Waltham, Massachusetts; Manfred Wengerek of Bedfordview, Transvaal; and Andrew Wilson of London.

Finally, my thanks to Stephen and Elke Day of Yalding, Kent, England for their German translations; to my wife, Lynn, who spent many hours transcribing taped interviews, researching, comparing notes, typing and encouraging; and to Liz Wilhide who edited the final manuscript with patience, great skill and understanding.

To all who helped in any way, my most grateful thanks. I need only add that the responsibility for any conclusions I have reached from information supplied by my helpers and friends is entirely my own.

EARL MOORHOUSE

Fifty Names

THE HIGHWAY STRETCHED four lanes wide toward Jan Smuts Airport. It was shortly before ten on Wednesday morning, November 20, 1974, and already the South African sun was blazing down harshly on the traffic rolling along the smooth freeway.

It was a beautiful morning and for Pat and Ian Horsfield and their three-year-old son, Timothy, of Johannesburg, it was a happy day. They were driving to the airport to meet Ian's sister, her husband and two young sons who had spent the last three months in Europe.

Their return was something of a surprise to the Horsfields. The Moorhouses' original plan had been to fly direct from Europe to Nairobi in Kenya, but there had been some difficulty with air tickets and yesterday Ian's brother-in-law had telephoned from Frankfurt, West Germany.

"Can you pick us up at the airport in the morning?" he had asked. "We can't get off in Nairobi so we're coming straight through."

"No problem at all," Ian had said. 'I'll take the day off. They owe me a few anyway."

So now they rode steadily along, cresting a hill, and saw the airport sprawled out flat in the distance. Ian noticed something briefly in his mirror, and a large American car roared wildly past, buffeting the slower moving Horsfields.

"Bloody idiot," Ian muttered as they watched the large car hurtling away from them.

As they drew into the airport carpark they saw the car again. It had just pulled into a parking space. The driver leaped out and ran wildly, dodging traffic, into the airport building. The Horsfields shook their heads, laughing. They got out of their car, took young Timothy by the hand and strolled over to the international terminal.

Inside the building they looked at the arrivals indicator board for flight LH540 from Frankfurt, but the flight was not listed. Ian Horsfield swore quietly.

"There's no damn plane there," he said. "The bloody Moorhouses must have been talking about tomorrow — and I've gone and taken the day off!"

They stood checking the flicking letters. Maybe it would still appear. But it didn't.

Ian said: "Let's go and ask at the information counter."

They walked over to the long desk in the international concourse. The woman working behind it looked up.

"Wasn't there supposed to be a Lufthansa flight arriving today?" Ian asked.

"Yes, there was." The woman spoke in a flat voice. "But it's been delayed."

"What do you mean, delayed? For how long?"

"Indefinitely."

"Indefinitely? What for?"

The Horsfields looked at each other, puzzled.

"Is there something wrong somewhere?" Ian asked. "Has something happened?"

"No," the woman said. "Look, why don't you phone Lufthansa? I don't know anything about it." She scribbled out the airline's Johannesburg number and handed it to them.

They looked around, saw a bank of public telephones nearby and went over quickly. Ian took up a telephone and started to dial. The number was engaged. He tried again. Engaged. Then, as he was dialing again, two men walked up, one with a camera slung from his neck.

"Excuse me," one of the men said. "I'm from the *Vaderland*."

"Oh, yes?" Ian looked at him.

"Were you waiting for someone on the Lufthansa flight?"

Ian felt himself suddenly go cold. He heard Pat cry out, "Oh God, no. Oh, no."

He said to the newsman, "What's happened?"

"Well —" the man hesitated. "Look, can I have an interview with you?"

"I'm not interested in an interview. What's happened? Has there been an accident?"

The newsman looked at Pat, then back at Ian. "Can I speak to you alone?"

"It's all right, you can speak in front of my wife. Has it crashed?"

"Yes," The newsman looked troubled, shook his head. "At Nairobi. We just heard that it had crashed. We don't —."

"How bad?"

The reporter shrugged. "We don't know. We were just told that it had crashed."

Ian ran back to the information desk.

"Look," he said to the woman, "I've just heard the Lufthansa plane has crashed. Do you know anything about it? Is anyone hurt? How bad is it?"

The woman shook her head. "I don't know. Phone Lufthansa. I don't know anything."

Ian turned in desperation to a second woman operating a switchboard behind the desk. "Please," he said, "can you get us a line to Lufthansa? We've tried the pay phone but we can't get through."

"All right, I'll try."

And they waited, tension mirrored in their faces, as the woman dialed out, got a busy signal, dialed again. Now, for the first time, they noticed the huddles of crying people in the concourse, the groups of reporters, the cameras. They had walked right through it all without seeing a thing. And they knew the unthinkable had happened. Some horror had befallen Flight LH540 and their relatives were aboard.

The switchboard operator looked up. "I've been trying over and over, but the lines are blocked."

"What do we do now?" Ian looked at Pat in a daze. Nothing prepared you for the absolute horror of it all. Then he thought of his younger brother, Robert, working for the Anglo-American Corporation in central Johannesburg. "Bobby," he said to Pat. "We'll phone Bobby. It'll take him seven or eight minutes to run down to the Lufthansa office. We can meet him there."

Pat nodded without speaking.

"You go and get some money for the phone while I try to get through to Bob."

Pat took Timothy by the hand and ran to the bank off the concourse. There were long lines of people at each teller's window and, frustrated by the slowness of everything, she felt like screaming, "Get out of my way! Get out of my way!"

It took her ten minutes to get to the teller. Then she scooped up the change and ran back to the telephones. A tall blond man rushed past her and grabbed a telephone handset. She saw tears in his eyes as he desperately dialed and dialed and dialed. She handed Ian a fistful of coins. He had just reached his brother.

"Look Bob," she heard him say, "take it easy now, but Lynn and Earl were supposed to be coming in on that Lufthansa flight this morning and we think it's crashed."

At the other end of the line in the center of Johannesburg, Robert Horsfield stood shocked. "Good God," he said hoarsely, thinking of his sister and her children and her husband. Gone? He felt sick to his stomach.

"Bob, we're still out here at the airport, but they can't tell us anything. And we can't get through to Lufthansa," he heard Ian saying. "Their lines are jammed."

Smoke billows from *Hessen* as firemen, rescue workers and the curious arrive at the scene of the crash. The ground is littered with the remains of a cargo of newspapers. (*East African Newspapers Ltd*)

(*above*) A dazed survivor is led from the burning wreck. The inflated escape chute can be seen in the background (*Stern*). (*below*) Numbed rescue workers kept at bay by the fierce heat which has reduced the plane to a twisted skeleton of molten metal

Robert Horsfield swallowed, listening. "Can you get down to their office and see what you can find out? We'll drive in right away and meet you there." "All right," Robert said and set down the phone. He felt dazed, looked round at the staring faces in his office. The color, his colleagues noticed, had drained from his face. "I've got to take an hour off," he said quietly. "My sister and her kids were in that jumbo that crashed." The office fell silent and everyone looked at Robert. The morning papers had headlined the crash across their front pages and there had also been reports on the radio. It was the world's first jumbo jet crash and the initial reports were awful. The jet had crashed in flames during takeoff from Nairobi Airport — as far as anyone knew, there were no survivors. But Robert, who had not seen a newspaper that morning or listened to the radio news, hadn't heard much about it. He had still been in bed when the jumbo had gone crashing down. Now he turned and dashed down the stairs, taking them two, three, four at a time.

He left the Anglo-American Corporation building and began to run along the street. After a block he slowed, walking quickly now, heart thumping in his chest, his suit sticking to him in the early morning heat as he went down the sidewalk. He shouldered through between pedestrians, crossed against the traffic lights, held his breath, walking, running blindly on through diesel fumes and smoke. He was trapped in a tunnel of horror. He had visions of his sister. He saw crashing jets in his mind. And then he pictured the smiling faces of those two children.

"Why?" he said to himself, remembering the last time he had seen them, three months ago, waiting that night at Jan Smuts Airport for their flight to Europe. They'd had drinks up in the lounge overlooking the runways. Through the glass of the windows they had looked down on the great jet shining in the floodlight and there had been laughing and joking and tears, because they'd always been like that, a close and emotional family, the men and the women. None of them could say hello or goodbye without a sudden showing of tears, but that night there had been more than tears. Pat had said, "I've got a feeling you won't be coming back, just a feeling that we won't see you again." Lynn had laughed lightly and said, "Oh, you will. You know us, we're always coming and going." Robert hadn't thought too much about it at the time, but now the words came back to him and hung heavily in his mind. Pat had known all along: She'd had a feeling, a presentiment, and now it had happened.

Robert pushed through the door of the Lufthansa offices and told the women behind the desk, "I've come about the crash. I've got family on board."

They sent him to an office upstairs. A man came through and spoke to him quietly.

"We've just heard from Nairobi. There are maybe fifty survivors. I'm sorry, we have no names. If you can leave your name and telephone number —"

Robert walked weakly back to the street. He felt a sudden despair. Only fifty. My God, what were the chances of even one of them surviving? What were the chances? Maybe one of them, there had to be one out of four. There just had to be. But which one? What if one of those boys had survived and was alone right now up there in Nairobi —

He stood on the sidewalk, staring desolately at the passing traffic, eyes burning, his throat tight. He swallowed hard. That survivor, if there was one, would need help.

Robert turned about and pushed into the airline office.

"I want to book a flight to Nairobi," he said thickly. "I want to go tonight."

The trip into Johannesburg was a hell ride. Pat Horsfield had never seen her husband so distraught. His face was white, he had gone all tense around his mouth and he was shaking his head as he drove, saying, "Oh my God, the kids, the kids —"

Three-year-old Timothy was protesting, "But I didn't see the plane land! Where's Garett and Brendon?"

Pat, staring out at the freeway, shook her head. "I don't know why, but I've got a feeling they're all right. I've just got a feeling."

"But what if Lynn and Earl are unconscious and the boys — maybe they've got no legs or something!"

"They're all right," said Pat. "I know they're all right."

But Ian was still shaking his head, hands clenching the wheel, and thinking, I can't believe this is happening, it can't be real, I must be dreaming. Any moment now I'll wake up. He reached out his hand like he'd read in books and pinched himself, hard, and felt it stinging and knew all of it was real.

"Oh my God," he said. "If a plane like that comes down — my God, if they survived they can't be in one piece."

The countryside, buildings, factories were slipping slowly by. Everything seemed to be happening in slow motion. It felt as if they would never get there. He watched the needle edging up on the speedometer.

"Don't speed," Pat told him. "It's not worth it. If we get stopped now — "

Yes, Ian thought grimly. I'd probably punch the bloody traffic cop. I haven't got the time or the patience to argue with anybody now.

"Those kids," he whispered and pictures of air crashes he'd seen in the past flashed suddenly through his mind. "My God, maybe they're burned."

Then the Horsfields were in the city. They found the Lufthansa office, parked in a no-parking zone — I don't care a damn, Ian thought — and ran in. It was the wrong office. They were told to go to another office round the corner on the fifth floor. They ran out.

A reporter stepped in front of them. "Excuse me — "

They brushed him aside, ran to the correct building, rode up the elevator, came out and walked into the Lufthansa administration offices. A woman in uniform looked at them. She was crying, her eyes red.

"We've come about the Lufthansa flight," Pat said.

"Who have you got on board?" She wiped her nose.

"My sister, her husband and two nephews," Ian said.

"Please come through." She led them to the next office. "He won't be a minute."

They sat and waited. The minutes ticked by. A uniformed man came through with a telex sheet in his hand.

"Will you please give me the name of your relatives."

"Moorhouse," the Horsfields said.

The man looked at his list. They saw his eyes moving. He looked further down. It seemed such a small piece of paper. Fifty names, that was all. Then his eyes stopped. He started to smile.

"Moorhouse," he read quietly, "G, B, E and L."

Pat and Ian took Timothy by the hand and caught the elevator back to the street. Out on the sidewalk they saw Robert walking toward them, his face taut with worry. Pat rushed to him and threw her arms around him, crying, "They're alive! We've just heard they're alive!"

And then, quite suddenly, everyone was crying.

Flight LH540

TUESDAY, NOVEMBER 19, 1974, was a cloudy day in Frankfurt, West Germany. Speeding in on the express train bringing us from the World Food Conference in Rome, I looked up at the low-lying clouds and thought, you're going to fly through that, you and Lynn and the two boys are going to fly through that. I was worried.

Then I thought, that's nonsense. It always feels like this on the day you fly and you always make it. I tried to put the thought out of my mind and consider instead the fascinating new life that lay ahead of us.

We were on our way to settle in Nairobi, Kenya, where I would work with the staff of the United Nations Environment Program as a liaison officer for the Friends of the Earth organization, which has groups in different parts of the world. Because it was a new post, a few guidelines had been drawn up, but the details had been left to me. On arrival in Nairobi, I would have to set up an office and a communications network and begin the long, gradual process of getting to know various key UN officials. It was an exciting prospect and we'd already had a foretaste during our three months of traveling around Europe. We'd financed the trip ourselves so we could meet the people and organizations I would be working for.

Back in Rome we'd tried to get Lufthansa to change our tickets so we could get off in Nairobi. We'd been traveling on excursion tickets and should have ended our trip back in Johannesburg where we had started, but it seemed pointless to go all that way when the flight would take us through Nairobi anyway. If the airline agreed, we argued, we'd get off there and save ourselves two takeoffs and landings — the worst part of flying — but our attempt failed.

When we arrived in Frankfurt that Tuesday morning we tried and failed again. An airline official explained that *we* could get off the plane, but our luggage would be labeled according to our tickets and would go on to Johannesburg. What would we do in Nairobi without luggage?

We shrugged, annoyed by the inflexibility of the system, and stepped out of the Lufthansa office into the cold and gray streets of Frankfurt.

Lynn squeezed my hand as I walked, collar up, into the wind. "*You* can always get off; they can't really stop you. I'll fly on with the boys and the luggage. I can spend the week with Pat and Ian in Johannesburg while you fix up everything in Nairobi, then we can fly up to meet you."

I thought about it. It was quite a good idea, but I wasn't sure. "Do you really want to?"

"I'd rather be with you," she smiled. "But it would save us some money and you'd save a few nerves."

"What about your nerves? No," I decided, shaking my head as we turned toward the train station, "we're all going together."

Sometimes, looking back, I feel sick thinking what might have happened if we had decided differently.

I made two calls from the international switchboard at the train station. One was to Lynn's brother, Ian Horsfield, in Johannesburg to ask him to meet us at the airport in the morning. He laughed, far away down the line in South Africa, and said: "Don't worry about it. I'll take the day off."

The other was to our friends, the Leslie-Melvilles, in Nairobi to tell them we'd be flying south through Nairobi in the morning, but we'd be back a week later. They were short calls because talking was expensive, but I felt good when I put down the telephone. We'd be out there with the Horsfields in the morning. I could see it already: blue skies, the boys splashing in the swimming pool, the rest of us relaxing in the sun . . . tomorrow!

"Come on," I picked up the baggage. "Let's get to that airport."

The train from Frankfurt to the airport roared into a tunnel and we were in darkness. The noise beat back off the wall, diminishing as the train slowed. There was a flash of light, we all blinked, and we had arrived at the airport station.

We climbed down off the train, loaded the baggage onto a trolley and pushed it down between the people toward the escalator. The trolley had a special fitting underneath so it could hook onto the moving staircase and the boys laughed as it caught and climbed the stairs with us. At the top the whole concourse opened up wide, bright and modern. We'd been here before so it was no longer a puzzle. Across the smooth floor we went, rolling the trolley ahead to the Lufthansa check-in desk.

I handed over the tickets and the ground stewardess stamped them; first the ticket of my wife, Lynn, then mine, then those of my sons Garett Jon, who was seven, and Brendon Scott, six.

"Where would you like to sit?" the stewardess asked.

I looked at my wife.

"In the nonsmoking section," she said.

The woman behind the desk smiled and handed over our boarding passes. She had seated us in row 26 between the wings on the port side of the Boeing 747: Brendon next to the window, Garett in the center seat, then myself. Lynn would sit in the first seat across the aisle.

The boys pushed the trolley to the baggage check. I picked up the cases and placed them on the scale. On the trolley stood my portable typewriter in its dark maroon traveling case. I picked it up.

"Will it be all right with the baggage," I asked the stewardess, "or should I take it with me?"

She nodded, laughing. "It'll be quite safe with the other things."

I put it on the scale and patted it. Another trip for you, old friend. Hands came up and lifted all of our luggage onto a conveyor belt.

I never saw the typewriter again.

Lufthansa's Flight LH275 from Milan had just landed and the jet wheeled in, engines shrieking, next to the terminal. Marketing coordinator Malcolm Solts, thirty-four, from Boston, Massachusetts, picked up his hand luggage and stepped off.

A few minutes later he was walking down a long airport corridor to the check-in desk. He had been on the go for weeks, it seemed, making great leaps across the globe. First, a flight across the Atlantic to Britain, and then a short hop over to France, then to Spain, Italy, and up to Germany to catch a long flight south to South Africa. It was business all the way, meeting after meeting with members of the far-flung Gillette company, different accents, different boardrooms. Thousands of miles in a few days, but he didn't think too much about it. It was almost a way of life.

The ground stewardess handed him his boarding pass, red for first class, and he tucked it safely away and headed for one of the businessmen's lounges. It was shortly after 4 P.M. and he had nearly five and a half hours before the flight left for Johannesburg.

Malcolm Solts got a drink from the bar, made himself comfortable in one of the chairs and spread out his papers. The lounge was a good, quiet place. He relaxed a moment, sipping at his drink, then took out his pen and started on his reports.

Hermann Hennecke spent the evening wandering about the shops on the concourse at Frankfurt Airport. Christmas was still five weeks away but there were gifts on sale that were impossible to find in Johannesburg and he knew his sons, Ulf who was ten and Ralf, seven, would be expecting "something special" from the toyshops of Europe. He smiled, thinking about them and his wife, half a world away, and guessed they'd be excited when they saw what he had in these packages.

He had been away for nearly two weeks, attending the budget talks of the Olympia Business Machines Company at Wilhelmshaven on the German North Sea coast in his capacity as managing director of the South African company. After the talks were over, he'd gone to spend the weekend with his parents at Bodenwerder in the Weser valley near Hannover and now he was on his way home. The thought of flying did not bother him. He already had one flight behind him that Tuesday evening: barely an hour before he had touched down aboard Lufthansa's Flight LH725 from Hannover.

Hermann Hennecke picked up his parcels and few items of luggage and walked across the smooth concourse floor to the Lufthansa check-in desk. He presented his ticket.

"Where would you like to sit?" the ground stewardess asked him.

"Somewhere in the center between the wings," he said. "It's smoother there. I'd like to get in a little sleep on the long flight, if that's possible."

"Certainly." The stewardess handed over a boarding pass. She had given him seat 4 in row 26.

"Thank you," he smiled. He would be able to see the movie and, if the jumbo wasn't too full, might even be able to kick his shoes off and stretch out over three or four seats. I'll be fresh when I get to Johannesburg, he thought, and almost in time for lunch.

He picked up his briefcase and headed for the international lounge.

The oldest person taking the flight was an eighty-eight-year-old inventor, Erich Hesse, who lived part of the year in West Berlin and the rest of the time in Bremervörde in northern Germany. He sat with his attaché case on his knees in the small departure lounge, his hands resting lightly on the case as he peered through his glasses at his fellow passengers around him.

He was determined not to let this case out of his sight. In it lay the precious papers that were his life's work — technical designs for wind-powered energy generation — and he did not want to lose them.

Hesse was flying to Johannesburg to celebrate his eighty-ninth birthday on December 26 with his daughter, Mrs. Gisela Hutton, his son-in-law, and his three young grandchildren. They were due to meet him at Jan Smuts Airport in the morning and drive him out to their suburban home in Linksfield. Until he got there he would keep this case as close to him as possible. Losing his papers now would be a disaster.

Forty-four-year-old Marie Galitzine of Paris was making her first trip to Africa as a Unitours travel company guide. A last-minute change of plans had put her in charge of a party of twelve Americans. The guide who had been scheduled for the trip had withdrawn and she'd been asked to fill the gap, despite the fact that she'd never been to Africa before. Until tonight she had only conducted tour groups around Europe.

Taking over this tour had meant canceling her own two-week holiday on the Riviera, but she didn't mind. She was fascinated by Africa and here, at last, she was within hours of seeing it.

Marie met the Americans for the first time in Frankfurt, a few hours before the flight was due to take off. They were a mixed group of four married couples and four single women who had flown over from the United States to Amsterdam and then on down to Frankfurt.

The oldest members of the group were Alfred and Veronica Solibakke, both seventy-seven, of Seattle, Washington — the home of the Boeing 747. The youngest in the party was Nancy Kahn who had just turned seventeen and was traveling with her parents, Karl and Renate Kahn of Dallas, Texas. Also from Dallas were Mrs. Tillie Harmel and her sister Mrs. Gladys Golman. Edmund and Elinor Senkler of Seattle, Elbert and Peggy Ottenheimer of Baltimore, and Mrs. Salome Zeiss from Pasadena, California were the other group members.

They had spent the day sightseeing in Frankfurt and got to the airport at about 8 P.M. Marie Galitzine was anxious to get the group checked in and their baggage weighed early. The group followed her to the Lufthansa desk, Karl Kahn helping the Solibakkes to load up a trolley with their things and wheel it along with the rest of the party. They were a relaxed bunch of people, laughing and chatting — thrilled at the prospect of seeing Africa in the morning.

Marie Galitzine slid herself up onto the baggage counter, swinging her feet, and invited them to choose their seats. They were all traveling on economy tickets, but there were different places they could sit. Up front, behind the first class section in the nose, was the quiet compartment where there would be no movie. Behind that and between the wings was the section for non-smokers and those who wanted to see the movie. And finally, stretching from row 32 about halfway down the long jet to the tail, was the smoking section where passengers could also see the movie.

The Unitours group divided itself into two. Marie Galitzine was a smoker and told her group that she would be sitting in the back. The other twelve tour members, including Nancy Kahn who was also a smoker, chose to sit in the nonsmoking section between the wings. Nancy would have to head for the tail section each time she felt like a cigarette, but she preferred to be near her parents and the rest of the group.

The check-in over, they wandered about the airport waiting for the flight to be announced. Karl Kahn, feeling the Solibakkes probably needed a helping hand, picked up their hand luggage and dropped it back on their trolley. Now all they had to do was wait.

Travel agent John Bing and his wife Jean, of Johannesburg, arrived at Frankfurt Airport loaded with Turkish souvenirs.

We look like Christmas trees with all our parcels, John Bing thought to himself as they walked through the airport building. They had collected most of their presents in Istanbul while attending the annual conference of the Universal Federation of Travel Agents' Associations a few days before. The meeting had been a memorable one for the Bings. John, already president of the South African Association of Travel Agents, had been elected chairman of the international body's African region. The election made him eligible for service on the board of directors. They stopped over in Frankfurt, guests of the German National Tourist Office, and collected some computerized accounts from the German Travel Agents' Association.

Now, at the check-in desk, they found they had been booked forward of the wings. They didn't like this position. Having flown thousands of miles in jumbos they knew the flight was smoothest over the wings and they asked to change their seats.

"Certainly," the ground stewardess said. She looked at her plan. "Where would you prefer?"

They pointed to the middle-wing area.

The stewardess wrote out their boarding passes. She had reseated them in row 31, the last of the seats in the nonsmoking section between the wings with the toilet cabinets behind them. The Bings gathered their parcels together. All they needed now was a half-empty flight so they could stretch out and sleep on the overnight leg to Nairobi. The last few weeks had been tiring and now they wanted to relax.

We had time to kill. I took Brendon for a walk to see the shops in the international lounge. A group of nuns passed by and smiled at him.

We walked on by a chapel; through the door I saw people praying.

"What's that?" Brendon asked.

"A church."

"A church at the airport?"

"Yes," I said.

"What for?"

"People like to pray before they fly. You can see some of the people in there now."

"Yes," he said, looking. "I can see three. What do they pray for?"

"For a safe journey, for God to look after the friends they're leaving behind. All sorts of things."

"Can we pray too?"

"If you like. Do you want to?"

"No," Brendon said. "Let's go back to Mama."

We walked back and Lynn said, "Where have you been? They're calling our flight."

"I'm sorry. We were looking at the shops."

I picked up the hand luggage and we walked in a group up the long corridor that led to our flight's departure lounge.

In the small departure lounge Hermann Hennecke toyed with his glasses as he waited for the flight to be called. He heard laughter, turned and saw a group of American tourists joking with each other. They were dressed casually, cameras and hand luggage slung over their shoulders, and looked like they were going on safari. Lucky people.

Hermann glanced at the others sitting around him: a group of nuns, couples with children, people whiling away the last few minutes with the day's newspapers. His eyes traveled on, took in the time on the digital clock. The figures were clicking steadily on toward 21.00 hours. We'll be lucky if we get away on time, he thought. Beyond the windows Lufthansa's Boeing 747, *Hessen*, glinted in the floodlights.

Bob Laburn, fifty-four, was one of the last to arrive at the lounge. The chief engineer of the Rand Water Board in Johannesburg looked through the doorway, saw the full seats and the groups of passengers milling about and decided to wait out in the passage. He turned back and sat on a bench next to a couple with a young child. They were smiling and talking quietly.

He was fiddling with his boarding pass as he waited and he thought back over the last few days in Europe. He had been to a conference of the International Water Suppliers' Association in West Berlin. The association's scientific and technical council met every two years and he was a chairman of one of the committees. It had been a short hard working trip with little time for relaxation and he felt a little tired and pleased to be heading home. It was all over for another two years.

He glanced at the seat number on his pass. Row 1. He would be sitting right up front in the first class section with a window at his right elbow. He always liked a window seat and always asked for one. Getting the first row right up in the nose was the luck of the draw.

Hans Neeb from Minden, near Hannover, sat watching the mothers with their young children and thought of his own wife and two young sons. By now they would be getting ready for bed, if they weren't there already. He smiled to himself and wished for a moment that he was back home instead of waiting here to make this journey halfway across the world.

He had flown the route four or five times a year since 1970 to spend a few weeks at the South African subsidiary of his firm, Eisenwerk Weserhütte, in Johannesburg. He had set up the subsidiary himself, was one of the directors and he liked to have first-hand knowledge of how it was getting on. He often took the night flight from Frankfurt, snatching a few hours' sleep and arriving in Johannesburg shortly before lunch.

Now as he waited, only minutes away from takeoff, he saw a business associate he knew rather well: Anthony Grant, the managing director of Southern Cross Steel and president of the Pretoria Portland Cement company. The two men shook hands and spoke briefly — there was a good deal they wanted to discuss.

"I'll come and see you after we've taken off," Hans Neeb told the South African businessman.

Mother Superior Dietlinde Geis, forty-six, was happy to be going. She was flying back to her mission work at the Holy Childhood Convent at Eshowe in Zululand after a home leave spent with the sisters of her "mother" convent at Würzburg-Oberzell in West Germany. While she waited she was surprised

and pleased to meet four other nuns from the Solanus Convent at
Landshut, not far from Munich: Sister Annuntiata Maier, sixty-
three, Sister Richardis Setzer, sixty-two, Sister Bona Hämmerle,
seventy-two, and Sister Blandina Hohenleitner, fifty-two. They
had also been on home leave and were now heading back to their
mission station at Harding in southern Natal where they had
worked for more than thirty years.

Mother Dietlinde did not belong to their order and had not met
them before, but they had a lot in common, and talked briefly
about their work. They were all a little excited. Tomorrow they
would be back with their people in the dry African heat.

Finally they parted, wishing each other a pleasant flight and
God's blessing for their continuing work. The four sisters returned
to their seats in the departure lounge and Mother Dietlinde sat
alone.

Her thoughts turned warmly to the hours and days she had
spent with the sisters of Würzburg-Oberzell. She would think of
them all with fondness and perhaps a little sadness in the days
ahead. And she would think of Germany, so far away.

Then it was time to board. Mother Dietlinde bowed her head as
the people began standing up and prayed, "God, protect this
flight." She sat awhile in silence, then she picked up her bags,
passed through the security check and boarded the aircraft.

Hermann Hennecke stepped through the narrow passageway
from the departure lounge into *Hessen*, and saw the soft lights,
the rows of seats stretching way back toward the tail, and the
stewardesses in their yellow jackets moving between the shuffling
passengers.

He handed over his boarding pass and a stewardess showed
him to his seat.

"Thank you," he nodded.

Hermann packed his parcels away in the overhead locker,
placed his briefcase on the seat next to him, sat down and buckled
himself in. The people were still filing in, but it was not so
crowded now, and he looked about feeling pleased with his

position. The aisle was one seat away to his right and there were empty seats all around him. The closest passenger was a young woman to his left. Across the far aisle sat what looked like the rest of her family, a man and two young boys.

He looked at his watch. Yes, they were a little late. The hands were edging on for 21.40, but they would probably make it up during the night.

Edmund and Elinor Senkler stepped into the jumbo jet and saw their fellow tourists Alfred and Veronica Solibakke already sitting there right close by the door.

"How did you manage to get such good seats?" Edmund asked as they passed. But the Solibakkes were not happy. They wanted to change their position, they told the Senklers, and later moved further forward.

The Senklers walked on down to their seats on the port side, strapped in and looked out at the lights glinting off the broad surface of the wing directly beneath them.

There was a fresh red rose waiting for each of *Hessen's* first class passengers as they were shown forward to their places in the jet's nose. The long-stemmed roses were attached to the seats by the stewardesses and were accompanied by the usual first class offerings: a pack of stationery, aircraft slippers for those who wanted to shed their shoes, a menu and a "welcome aboard" cocktail of champagne and orange juice. After takeoff would come more free drinks, cigars and cigarettes, a gourmet dinner, chocolates, cognac and liqueurs.

Bob Laburn settled himself and fastened his seat belt. To his right was the window he had asked for and through it he could see the lights of the airport and the small vehicles moving about the runway. The man in the twinned seat next to him did not introduce himself and, probably because they spoke different languages, they did not try to talk to each other.

Also in the first class section sat West German Bundestag Vice-President Liselotte Funcke and three other Bundestag members, Dr. Curt Becker, Dr. Rolf Böhme and Mr. Rudolf

Rescue workers cope with the appalling tragedy as explosions continue
to shake the jet

Flight Engineer Rudi Hahn, gripping a dislocated shoulder, is helped away from the wreck. (*East African Standard*, Nairobi)

Müller, who would disembark at Nairobi in the morning to begin an official visit to Kenya.

Globe-trotting Malcolm Solts had an aisle seat four rows from the front on the left side of the aircraft. He had asked for a seat in the nonsmoking section and this was what the stewardess had given him, a seat not far from the staircase that wound up to the first class cocktail lounge.

He sat waiting for the jet to move off and looked about him, seeing his fellow passengers for the first time. He had worked steadily on his reports throughout the afternoon and into the evening, closed off in the lounge from the usual preflight crowds, and then he had taken a walk around the duty-free shops to buy gifts for his family. He had not met any other passengers until he got aboard, but there was little time for conversation now. It was almost time to go.

Outside the engines began howling and, looking down, I saw the workmen moving in the half-light below. The sound of the engines changed and the airport building began to swing away. The big jet was taxiing.

At the head of the runway the engines built to a roar, the jet bobbed a little and then, whoosh, we were off, hurtling down the runway. I looked left and saw the lights going flash-flash by. The buildings were blurring past. Faster, faster, I said in my mind and a strange daredevil feeling took over. We could all go up in flames if something went wrong, yet here I was gambling with life, exhilarated by the surging power, the race toward oblivion — or takeoff. Come on, get there, my mind shouted. Get there! The lights were streaming past, the nose lifted, there was a jerk, air under the wheels, and then we were off, screaming slowly up against gravity.

Thrust back in the seat, I willed the plane on. The critical moment passed, we rose into the night sky and the lights of Germany were falling away below.

I looked across the aisle at Lynn. She looked at me, sighed and smiled.

It was time for cocktails. Hermann Hennecke sat nursing a Bloody Mary, and started reading the paperback detective novel he had bought at Frankfurt Airport. He didn't have long to read: soon there was a rattling of trays and the cabin staff came quickly down the aisle with the heated-up dinners and placed one on his folded-down seat-tray. Hermann smoothed out his paper napkin and began to eat.

It was a smooth and pleasant flight. There was almost no turbulence, only the steady pulsing of the engines. Hermann ate on, feeling relaxed. He was looking forward to the Clint Eastwood movie to while away an hour or so. *Dead End* was an odd title, but he guessed it would be lively enough. Eastwood movies usually were.

He looked to his left and smiled at the young woman sitting a seat away. She was nibbling a dry cracker and a cup of tea stood next to the pack on the tray in front of her.

"I can't eat anything when I'm flying," Lynn Moorhouse told him.

Hermann nodded. "Are those your two boys over there?"

She looked across the aisle at her husband and two young boys tucking into the big dinner. "Yes," she said. "Garett and Brendon."

"They must be about the same age as my two boys. They even look like them."

"Oh, they all look alike at this age. I don't know why." She smiled and bit at her cracker.

They lapsed into silence and didn't speak again until it was all over.

At row 38 toward the rear of the aircraft Hans Neeb and Anthony Grant held their long in-flight business discussion. They were deeply involved in their conversation and did not pay any attention to the antics of the young children in the next aisle, or to the nuns or any of their other fellow passengers.

The arrival of dinner brought them back to their surroundings. A stewardess was handing out the trays. Hans Neeb stood up in the aisle, feeling he would have liked to have spoken a bit longer to his business friend. There was so much to talk about.

"Perhaps we can continue our discussion tomorrow morning between Nairobi and Johannesburg," he suggested and Anthony Grant agreed.

Hans Neeb edged past the stewardesses, smiled a greeting at Mr. John Hall, general manager of Southern Cross Steel who was sitting a row ahead of Anthony Grant, and headed back toward his seat in the economy class. He had a fairly long walk to his seat in the quiet compartment directly behind the first class section.

The dinner trays were stacked away and in the dim after-dinner light passengers prepared to watch Clint Eastwood on the screen. They would hear the soundtrack through earphones; others could ignore the movie and listen instead to six channels of prerecorded music, they could read, or they could simply doze fitfully while the jet rumbled through the night.

Malcolm Solts, sitting in the first class section, didn't feel like watching the movie. He had spent the early part of the flight reading and then chatting to the German couple from Düsseldorf who were seated behind him. The man, he guessed, was about fifty and had told him they were going to South Africa to visit friends and spend some time in the sun. It had been pleasant talking to them, swapping stories, smiling a bit, and whiling away the time before dinner and now that dinner was over, he didn't feel like staring at Clint Eastwood.

Solts got up, stretched his legs, and climbed the stairs to the cocktail lounge on the upper deck. It was perhaps the closest airplanes had come to matching the luxury of the great ocean liners — a lounge in the sky.

He got a drink, sat himself down in an upholstered chair and spoke to a woman sitting nearby. She told him she was originally from England, but was now living in Germany and working for an accounting firm. Tonight she was on her way to Johannesburg for a business meeting.

They talked on. Beyond the portholes of the lounge the stars shifted slowly in the dark of the sky. And down in the cabin below Clint Eastwood smiled grimly, chasing after his busload of hijacked children.

Much later someone came up the stairs. Malcolm Solts looked up and saw the German who had been sitting in the seat behind him.

"May I join you?" he asked.

"Certainly."

He got himself a drink and came over, and they sat there talking and drinking, three strangers drawing closer and closer to Nairobi with each sweeping second.

Renate Kahn from Dallas, Texas, could not relax or get to sleep. She wandered down to the rear of the aircraft and sat talking with tour guide Marie Galitzine. Renate thought she was charming and delightful and would guarantee the success of their African tour. Marie seemed to make friends easily and already had all her tour-group members calling her "Maya." Several of them, including Nancy Kahn, had come to the back to have a drink or smoke with her, or simply to pass the time chatting.

While she was in the tail section Renate Kahn also met and spoke to children's stewardess Helge Nachtsheim who was entertaining a group of about six youngsters while their parents watched the movie. She was known as the "Mickey Mouse" because of the large smiling Disney character she wore on the front of her uniform. Lufthansa's route to South Africa was the only one that offered this service. To become a "Mickey Mouse," Helge told Renate, you had to be able to speak German and English and you had to be a mother. Helge satisfied both requirements — back home in Johannesburg she had sons of two and eleven who were being looked after by a relative.

She had been kept busy on tonight's flight, reading and playing games with the children, and she had a hunch she would probably be busy right through the night. But she didn't mind. She enjoyed looking after them and they seemed to like being with her.

This flight was different from other flights she'd made, Helge said and smiled toward the man sitting at the back of the aircraft — her husband Klaus. He had been on a business trip to Germany and had hired Elke Stosch, a thirty-year-old interpreter from Düsseldorf, as a secretary for his firm in Johannesburg. They had worked together in Germany several years ago, before the Nachtsheims emigrated to South Africa.

Klaus had arranged his trip so they could all be on the same flight going home and had even managed to get two seats next to Helge's so they could sit together. But the "Mickey Mouse" didn't use her seat for much more than takeoffs and landings. She was too busy. Most of the time, she told Renate Kahn, she was on her feet with the children.

Clint Eastwood had chased the kidnapper to a bloody death. The screens faded as the movie ended and now there was only music or sleep. But Renate Kahn was still restless and wandered about the aircraft.

Earlier, after takeoff from Frankfurt, she had toured the cabin looking for two or three unoccupied seats in a row where her daughter Nancy could stretch out for the night. Eventually, in the rear section, she had found two alongside the group of nuns and placed coats on them to show that they had been taken.

But Nancy Kahn wasn't interested in sleeping that night, and after a while she suggested to her mother: "Why don't you go and take the coats and things off those seats so someone else can have them?"

"Are you sure?"

"I really don't feel like sleeping," Nancy told her.

Renate turned back to remove the coats and noticed a nun sitting many rows away from the others, in a completely different area of the jumbo. Perhaps she would like to take over those seats, Renate thought.

She went up to the nun and said to her in German, "Your sisters are sitting in the back and I've found some empty places right next to them. Wouldn't you prefer to be with them? You might enjoy sitting there and stretching out for the night. There's plenty of space."

The nun smiled and thanked her. Yes, she would like to be with the others. She got up, picked up her bag and walked with Renate to the seats still draped with the coats alongside her fellow sisters.

Renate picked up the coats and the nun sat down and made herself comfortable, smiling at Renate.

"Thank you very much," she said. "You are very kind."

Well, Renate thought heading back to the seats where Karl Kahn lay dozing, at least I've made someone happy. I hope she can manage to sleep.

It was quiet in the big jet, the lights were dimmed and the plastic slides had been drawn down over the windows. *Hessen* had flown high over the Alps, crossed southern Europe and the darkened Mediterranean, and thrust on now through the sky like an arrow above the vast sleeping African plains.

Hermann Hennecke kicked off his shoes and stretched out on the empty seats. He had a pillow under his head and drew the blankets up under his chin. For a while he listened to the hissing of the air conditioning, felt the gentle bobbing as the jet powered ahead, and then he fell fast asleep.

An African Departure

IT WAS RAINING in Nairobi. The drops fell in long lines past the neon lights shining from the hotel rooftops, splashed heavily into the night-darkened streets and swirled away down the gutters and drains. And beyond the city, in the open fields and bush, rain turned the earth into a thick mud that clung to boots and shoes and feet and wheels.

In a room at the Intercontinental Hotel, not far from the towering Kenyatta Conference Center in the heart of the city, nine Lufthansa cabin crew members sat talking and joking and laughing. Their three-day rest period was drawing to a close and they had been invited to while away the last few hours before bed in the room of Captain Norbert Diekmann, a twenty-three-year-old German Federal Border Guard who had been seconded to Lufthansa in Nairobi as a security officer.

He got on well with the flying crews, driving them around the city, showing them the sights, fetching and carrying. But this particular crew was even better than usual — a swinging crowd, he thought. They had arrived in Nairobi in the early hours of Sunday morning aboard a 747 from Frankfurt and looked pretty tired. But after a few hours' sleep they soon recovered and by the next afternoon were making plans for an all-night party.

The party, held on Monday night at the home of a German businessman friend, was a great success. The talking, dancing and drinking went on until the early hours and only ended when the stewards and stewardesses straggled back to their rooms at the Intercontinental. One or two of them even managed a nightcap up in Norbert Diekmann's room.

But tonight, because they were due to take off for Johannesburg shortly before eight in the morning, there was no drinking. Lufthansa's regulations prohibited any crew member from drinking alcohol twelve hours before a flight.

Instead, they took it easy, relaxing on the hotel furniture and talking among themselves. They would still have another two rest days in Nairobi when they got back from Johannesburg aboard Wednesday night's northbound flight. They were all looking forward to it — another two days in Nairobi and, with luck, the sun would be shining all the time.

In a different room at the Intercontinental the fifty-three-year-old crew commander for tomorrow's flight, Captain Christian Krack, was getting ready for an early night's sleep. He had returned that afternoon from a wildlife safari with his wife Erika and his daughter Karin in a rented Volkswagen. They had flown out from Germany on the Saturday flight, slept off the initial effects at the hotel on Sunday morning, and then driven northwest, taking the road that runs along the floor of the Rift Valley to Lake Navaisha. There they had spent the night before traveling on the next morning, heading southwest to the Keekorok Lodge. They spent hours driving across the rolling plains of the Masai Mara Reserve, searching out the lions, elephants, rhinos and herds of buffalo that migrated northward across the Tanzanian border from Serengeti. After a night at the lodge they traveled back to Nairobi the next afternoon.

The three-day safari had been a relaxed and happy time for the Kracks, and especially for Karin. This trip to Africa was a birthday gift from her father. Tomorrow, Wednesday, November 20, she would be twenty-two. And in the morning, while her father flew the incoming 747 south to Johannesburg, she and her mother planned to go bargain-hunting in the shops of Nairobi.

Fifty-year-old Flight Engineer Rudi Hahn was already in bed and drifting slowly off to sleep. He had spent a good deal of his three-day rest period working on his income tax declaration in his hotel room and the hours of paperwork had tired him out. He didn't think much about the morning's flight. In his career he had already notched up 13,236 flying hours, 2,650 of them on Boeing jumbo jets, and felt quite relaxed about it all. He had been flying for Lufthansa since 1955, first on Lockheeds and then on Boeing 707s and 727s, and was finally checked out for duty on 747s in March 1971.

The flight engineer was in good physical shape and felt well. He had sailed through his last medical check just over four months ago. His licence was endorsed "Holder to carry reading glasses," but he only really needed to use them when his eyes were tired or when the light was poor. That did not happen often and rarely in Africa. The chances were he would not need them for tomorrow's flight.

The on—off rain had kept the copilot, First Officer Hans-Joachim Schacke, in the hotel for most of the three-day break. But he wasn't particularly interested in rushing about "having fun." He had been to Nairobi twelve times already and felt he had done nearly all the things and seen all the sights the city had to offer. This visit he preferred to take things easy and stay around the hotel.

Schacke was thirty-five and had flown Starfighters for the West German Air Force before joining Lufthansa in 1968. The airline started him as a copilot on Boeing 727s and switched him to Boeing 747s in 1971 after he had undergone conversion training. Since then he'd clocked up 2,237 hours as a jumbo copilot. Only a few of those hours had been in the company of Captain Krack;

the first time had been a week ago when they flew a Lufthansa freight jumbo between Frankfurt and New York.

Tomorrow's takeoff would be his thirteenth from Embakasi Airport out there on the fields beyond the city. The copilot turned out the light and tried to sleep.

At. 5.15 that Wednesday morning, while semidarkness still hung over the city of Nairobi, the seven men and ten women who made up the relief crew for *Hessen* were woken up. In their different rooms up in the Intercontinental Hotel they took out their uniforms and started to dress — dark navy blue uniforms for the men and bright yellow summer outfits for the women. When they had dressed they packed a few items they would need for their short stay in the "golden city" of Johannesburg.

Captain Krack went through and wished his daughter a happy birthday, said goodbye to his wife and went down to the hotel lobby to meet his crew. Copilot Schacke arrived and Krack saw Flight Engineer Hahn coming in. They both looked rested although Schacke felt he hadn't slept too well. They stood quietly together, the three men who, in a few minutes, would be at the controls of *Hessen*. The cabin crew began to assemble as the Captain stared out through the glass front of the hotel, watching for the two Volkswagen minibuses that would ferry all of them out to Embakasi.

The buses turned quickly into the hotel yard and drew up outside the entrance. The cockpit crew picked up their hand luggage and walked out, and behind them straggled the cabin crew. Some of the crew were a little late and came running up behind. Heidi Tischer, a purser, scolded the latecomers and after some lighthearted banter they were all seated in the buses. The engines revved and the leading bus nosed out of the hotel parking area onto the road, with the second bus close behind. They wheeled left and accelerated down the Uhuru Highway, past the Kenyan Parliament Buildings, climbed the hump over the railway line, and purred smoothly along the Mombasa road in the direction of the airport.

The light was improving all the time, the early morning mist slowly dispersing and the somber sky brightening. The buses drove steadily on, the wheels splashing through puddles on the still-wet road. A sign pointed to the airport. They swung off left and far ahead the crew saw the terminal building.

The minibuses drew up to the airport entrance and the crew of seventeen picked up their bags and strolled into the building, walked through the concourse and down a passageway to the room where they would have their final preflight briefing. Somewhere, way out beyond the bush, *Hessen* was making its approach.

Back in Nairobi, a third minibus toured the streets, calling at hotels to take passengers to Embakasi Airport. Margaret Hooker, waiting with her baggage at her hotel, saw it drawing up outside and stepped out to board it. She was anxious to be on her way after her overnight stop in the Kenyan capital. She felt she was racing against time. Her mother, seventy-seven-year-old Mrs. Maggie Laing, was lying seriously ill in Cape Town, South Africa, and the family was worried she would not survive to celebrate her seventy-eighth birthday on December 3.

The day before, Margaret had said goodbye to her civil engineer husband David in Jeddah, Saudi Arabia, and boarded a Pakistani Airlines flight to Nairobi. This morning she was due to fly south to Johannesburg where she would be met by her brother, break her journey briefly, and then fly on to her mother's bedside in Cape Town.

She got onto the bus and saw there was only one other passenger on it, a woman about her age, and as the bus started on its ride through the city to the airport they began talking. The other woman was American-born Carol Mall, forty-seven, who had been working in Addis Ababa, Ethiopia, for the Agency for International Development, which administers the foreign aid program of the United States government. She was on vacation, she told Margaret Hooker, and she had decided to visit Cape Town and Johannesburg.

"Johannesburg?"

Carol Mall nodded and Margaret thought about the city she knew so well and wondered where Carol would go and what she would do in a place like that. It was such a big sprawling city and it could get terribly lonely for a woman on her own.

"Look," she said to Carol Mall, "I'm going to be staying for a time with my sister in Germiston. That's almost the same city. You tell me where you are and I'll phone you so we can arrange something."

They swapped numbers and addresses, talking on as the bus drove out across the flat countryside, and by the time it drew up outside the airport terminal they were already good friends.

Fifty Minutes to Live

DAWN BROKE ABOARD *Hessen* and down below were the yellow-brown fields of Africa. The passengers who had been sleeping opened their eyes and stretched.

Elinor Senkler had spent the night on two empty seats in the tail section and got up when she heard the clatter of breakfast trays. Everyone back there looked a bit rumpled and there were blankets and pillows over the seats, and shoes and bags and belongings strewn over the floor. Only the nuns, sitting upright in their dark habits, looked neat and collected — a picture of serenity in the shambles around them.

Looking back, Elinor saw a young mother sitting at the rear of the jumbo with a sleepy child on her lap. Fussing about between her and the other children was "Mickey Mouse," Helge Nachtsheim, still looking cheerful after the long night. The stewardesses came down the aisles offering a prelanding snack, but many just settled for a cup of hot coffee.

Elinor gathered up her things and walked back to rejoin her husband Edmund in the economy compartment. She sat down and buckled in. They would soon be landing.

Minutes later, the seat belt signs came on and there was an

announcement about smoking. The jet dropped steadily and down below the passengers could see the buildings of Nairobi and ribbons of roadways against the earth. Shortly before 7 A.M. the jumbo came skimming in over the bush and touched down gently on the runway at Nairobi Airport. The jet shook as the engines went into reverse thrust. It was a beautiful landing, so smooth that passengers broke into applause.

The jet taxied off to the service area, turned, was guided in by a man with markers, and stopped. The engines shut off and the vibration that had been there all the way from Frankfurt was suddenly gone. The steps came rolling up, the doors were swung open, and silence flooded in.

When the briefing was over the new crew members stepped out of the airport building onto the runway. There, glinting in the light, stood *Hessen*, a huge jet, towering high above the service vehicles, dwarfing all the other aircraft waiting on the apron.

The cabin crew walked together down toward the plane, bags slung over their shoulders, some carrying hand baggage. The two sets of steps were up next to the doors and a catering vehicle came past.

Then, in the pale early morning sun, something happened that lodged in the mind of Tom Scott, a dark-haired twenty-four-year-old American-born steward whose initial three months of probation with the airline were coming to an end. Four members of the cabin crew ran out ahead with cameras and turned like a party of tourists to photograph their friends. There were smiles and grins and a bit of face-pulling as Manfred Vohs, twenty-seven, Rolf Nietser, twenty-eight, Renate Kriegleder, twenty-four, and twenty-two-year-old Rita Selbach snapped away. It was unusual and unexpected, but Tom Scott didn't think too much about it then. Later, the incident would replay itself vividly in his mind over and over again.

Captain Krack and his crew waited at the foot of the forward gangway and peered up at the doorway as the disembarking passengers started coming down. This morning the crew had with them Dr. Harald Heimsoeth, the West German ambassador to

Kenya, who was there to welcome the four Bonn Parliamentarians at the start of their official visit.

Down the gangway they came, led by Vice-President Liselotte Funcke, shook hands and were escorted away by Dr. Heimsoeth. More passengers followed, and finally, the crew that had flown *Hessen* through the night from Frankfurt. The two captains greeted each other and Captain Krack was told: no defects or difficulties. *Hessen* was in excellent shape.

The relief crew went aboard. Captain Krack, First Officer Schacke and Flight Engineer Hahn went forward to the first class compartment, climbed the staircase to the cocktail lounge and entered the cockpit through the connecting door. On the deck below, the cabin crew took up their positions by the doors — a safety precaution in case the aircraft caught fire during refueling and they had to evacuate the passengers.

Tom Scott stood by the open doorway immediately forward of the port wing with Check Purser Jürgen Freund who was on the flight to check his performance and that of the other two probationers, Christel Pilz, twenty-four, and Monika Spiegl, twenty. All the working positions for the flight had been decided by drawing lots before they left Frankfurt on Saturday night, and they would keep to them throughout the African journey. Tom Scott had drawn this position alongside the small kitchen where they heated meals and would share the twin fold-down seats in the doorway with Jürgen Freund during the takeoff. They would strap in facing the tail shortly before the roll began.

The four crew members who had taken pictures on the apron had drawn positions way back in the tail compartment. They had fifty minutes to live.

The Kahn family were up and walking around the aircraft soon after it had stopped out on the apron. They saw the new crew come aboard and take up their positions by the doors and then Nancy became absorbed in lacing up her hiking boots. They were big and comfortable and she'd brought them along because she figured they'd be doing a lot of rough walking in Africa. She had kicked them off during the night and walked around the aircraft in her socks but now, on landing, she put them back on. We might get off the plane, she thought.

But the Kahns didn't get off. The stop was too short and they would be coming back to Nairobi in a few weeks anyway. It didn't seem worth the trouble just to see the airport. All airports looked about the same. So Nancy left her boots on.

Her father, Karl Kahn, had spent the night stretched out on the center section seats and had slept for several hours. Now he took himself off to the toilets for a wash. He found one empty, went in, washed and even managed to shave before there was a hammering on the door. He opened up, surprised, and saw a Kenyan standing outside with dusters and brooms.

"Please, sir," he said. "I have to clean now."

Karl picked up his few things and headed back to his seat. The caterers were carrying food aboard in cartons and there were other people wandering about. Karl sat down in his seat and checked to see if he still had all his photographic equipment. His 35-mm camera and his movie camera were there under his seat, and he got up and moved across the aisle to a window. He had been allocated a window seat at Frankfurt but had crossed the aisle to spread out for the night. Now, with luck, he might get some aerial shots of Kilimanjaro. Nancy sat down next to him and they waited together for takeoff.

Renate Kahn used the stopover to stretch her legs. While she was strolling about she was surprised to see "Mickey Mouse" Helge Nachtsheim still aboard.

"I thought the crew changed here in Nairobi," Renate said.

Helge Nachtsheim nodded. "Yes, the regular crew does. But I'm only the "Mickey Mouse" and I've got to fly all the way to Johannesburg. I'm not really a member of the crew."

"That's a long trip."

"Yes, it is," the children's stewardess agreed. "But I don't really mind. And I have my husband with me this time."

Renate watched her walk back down to the tail compartment. Helge looked tired. She must have had a long and busy night.

Hans Neeb had meant to go back and continue his business

(*above*) The crash site—in the foreground the remnants of an aircraft
seat. (*below*) The burning fuselage with an engine lying in the foreground.
(*Van Hoef*, Brussels)

The fire over, pieces of wreckage are left where they fell for expert investigation (*East African Standard*, Nairobi)

discussion with Anthony Grant in the rear section of the jumbo during the stopover. But he never got there. As he stood in the open doorway, breathing in the fresh Kenyan air, he heard a voice he knew. He looked around and saw a German colleague of his, Dr. Gerd Kampf-Emden, and the two men shook hands, surprised but happy to see each other. Dr. Kampf-Emden was flying first class to Johannesburg to take up his new position as the managing director of a German company.

They discussed working in Africa and Hans Neeb was enthusiastic. Dr. Kampf-Emden would find it most enjoyable, he predicted, and it wasn't as far from Europe as it seemed — just an overnight flight away. You could leave your office in Germany in the afternoon, sleep on the plane, arrive in Johannesburg shortly before midday and still manage to get in a good afternoon's work.

They chatted on, watching the airport workmen fussing over the jet, and made an arrangement to meet again in Johannesburg.

Elinor Senkler stood at the doorway and looked out at Africa for the first time. She saw gray clouds with the sun struggling through, a vast flat landscape of dull grass and small thorn trees and, way off in the distance, a few lonely trees.

She was surprised by what she saw; it didn't fit the mental picture she'd had of Africa. Somehow she had expected it to be more lush, the vegetation denser and more like a jungle, but here was flat open grassland verging on semidesert. This was Nairobi, right on the equator, where it was supposed to rain all year round.

She looked around to see what others were making of it and saw fellow-travelers Alfred and Veronica Solibakke seated not far away in the quiet compartment of the economy section. Veronica Solibakke was standing over her husband and combing out his thinning hair. Elinor watched, smiling to herself. It was a peaceful, domestic sort of scene you expected to see at home, not here on the apron of an African airport.

I looked out to port, saw the fuel line attached to the wing, the men working out there with the red Nairobi Airport Fire Brigade tender close by, and I felt fear in my stomach. All that fuel going in and here we sat. All it needed was a spark and this machine would explode like a bomb. I felt so terribly vulnerable and insignificant, watching the figures out there beyond my young sleeping son. My mouth felt dry. I looked across at Lynn and smiled.

"It's damn hot."

She nodded.

I unbuckled my seat belt, stood up and placed my jacket in the locker overhead. In the pockets were my passport, a notebook and pens. I took out the small pillows, dropped one down onto Garett's legs, kept one, and snapped the locker shut.

"What's this for?" Garett asked.

"For takeoff," I said. "In case we bump our heads."

I strapped him in, arranged the pillow on his knees, and sat back to buckle myself in. I pulled the belt tight, very tight, the pillow resting on my thighs.

Nothing to do but wait. I reached out for the safety instruction sheet kept in the string bag behind each seat and studied the position of the safety exits. It was something I did before each takeoff. My God, I hated takeoffs.

Then I slipped it back and leaned back in the seat. My palms were sweating on the pillow.

Margaret Hooker and Carol Mall climbed up the gangway into the big jet. A stewardess showed them to their places in the front row of the economy seats immediately behind the first class compartment and they settled themselves and strapped in for takeoff. They were in a three-seater, Margaret right up against the leftside window, a vacant seat between them, and Carol on the aisle.

Back in the airport terminal the man allocating seats had glanced at the diagram showing him the vacant places and had given them two numbers. Then he'd hesitated.

"Wait a minute," he said. "Would you two ladies like to sit together?"

"Yes," they said because they had already struck up a conversation and seemed to get on well together.

The airline man looked back at his plan.

"As close to the toilet as possible," Carol said. "I've got an awful stomach bug."

"I think we can manage something." He gave them two new numbers and when they got on board they found they were only about two steps away from the first class toilet cabinets.

Up in the cockpit Captain Krack and his two flight deck colleagues were planning *Hessen*'s takeoff while the ground crew down below pumped in the last of the 61,000 kilograms (134,481 lbs) of fuel the 747 would carry. There were 157 people aboard, including the crew, and a quantity of freight and baggage, making up a total estimated takeoff weight of 254,576 kilograms (561,236 lbs) — well below the aircraft's maximum authorized level. Because of this, the commander decided to follow the usual practice of planning a takeoff using reduced engine power.

The throttle setting would be −3A power. This setting meant that *Hessen* would need 2,484 meters (2,717 yds) of runway for its takeoff roll if it used runway 06, or 2,789 meters (3,051 yds) if it used runway 24. The actual length of the 06/24 runway was 4,117 meters (4,504 yds) and the plane could take off safely in either direction.*

Copilot Schacke, sitting in the right-hand pilot's seat, began reading the cockpit and the preliminary checklists with the various crew members responding. He had been designated the handling pilot for the sector.

Next to him sat Captain Krack, who was wearing his bifocals. He had taken off from Nairobi ten times before and knew the airport well. He was one of Lufthansa's most experienced pilots, transferring to the airline in 1957 after serving as a pilot in the Federal Air Force. Initially he flew as a copilot and later as a captain on Lockheed 10490 and Corvair 440 aircraft and switched to Boeing 707s and 727s in 1966. In May 1972 he was checked out as a captain of Boeing 747 aircraft and had flown

---

* At the time of the accident, Nairobi Airport had a single asphalt runway designated 06/24. Runway 24, the direction used by *Hessen*, had an average uphill slope of 0.4 percent. Using this runway and −3A power, the maximum permissible takeoff weight would have been approximately 284,000 kilograms (626,108 lbs).

1,619 hours in them. His total flying experience was 10,464 hours and about 8,000 of those hours had been flown as a commander.

At 7.42 A.M. the engines were started using a revised procedure the airline had introduced late in 1973. The bleed valves, which pass air from the engines to the pneumatic system to extend the leading edge wing flaps, were to be switched to the closed position. Once the engines had been started, the flight engineer was expected to reopen the bleed valves, restoring the power that would automatically extend the leading edge flaps when the copilot signaled the flaps to move into the takeoff position. Fully extended leading edge flaps are almost essential for a successful takeoff, especially at high-altitude airports like Nairobi.* They increase the area of the wings and help to create the "lift" that enables the aircraft to overcome the pull of gravity.

On this morning, making the "after-start" check, the engines roaring, copilot Schacke called out: "Bleed valves."

There was a short pause and Flight Engineer Hahn answered: "Open," signifying that he had also checked the indicator lights on his panel which show the position of the valves.

This was the expected response. The check continued normally.

The passengers who had boarded in Nairobi had stowed away their hand luggage and were strapping in for the flight to Johannesburg. It was obvious they had just got on from the restless way they sat, fidgeting, looking around them, trying out the push buttons on the armrests, talking brightly. The others who had stayed on board during the fifty-minute stop sat dozing in their seats, belts buckled, trying to make up the sleep they'd missed during the night.

Tom Scott closed the door next to him, swung the handle and sealed it. He made his checks, felt satisfied, and sat down on his seat. The jumbo was vibrating gently.

---

* Prior to the Nairobi accident, a number of Boeing 747 aircraft took off successfully with the leading edge flaps wholly or partly retracted. But it is believed that all these takeoffs occurred at lower altitude airfields than Nairobi (5,000 feet). It is also possible that the takeoffs were made at higher levels of power than that used by *Hessen* at Nairobi, although no information on this is available.

At 7.48$\frac{1}{2}$ A.M. the Control Tower called to the *Hessen* crew: "Lufthansa five four zero. Nairobi Tower."

"Five four zero," copilot Schacke acknowledged. "Go ahead."

"Roger. You may take runway two-four at your discretion or runway zero-six. Your choice."

"Oh-two-four, okay?" Captain Krack said. Using runway 24 would give *Hessen* a shorter flight path to the final flight track to Johannesburg.

"We take two-four," Schacke informed the Tower.

"Roger. Cleared to taxi holding point, runway two-four."

"Roger," the copilot said into his microphone. "We are cleared to holding point, runway two-four. Are we cleared to enter?"

Captain Krack made some comment that was later indecipherable on the flight recorder.

Then at 7.49$\frac{1}{2}$ A.M. the Tower broke in: "Lufthansa five four zero. That is approved. Enter and backtrack."

"Roger. Thanks," copilot Schacke said. "So, the flaps."

"Yes," the commander agreed.

There was a chattering noise as the copilot set the flaps to the 10 degrees takeoff position. On a normal flight, this lowering of the trailing edge flaps would automatically have signaled the vital leading edge flaps to extend. But if the bleed valves were closed there would be no pneumatic power to make this happen.

"So, that goes out pretty straight."

The flight crew spoke briefly about the weather, the cockpit's four-channel voice recorder struggling to pick up their voices through the area microphone in the roof. The other three channels were linked to the individual crew members' intercom phones which they were not using on this morning's flight, preferring to speak directly to each other.*

A little later First Officer Schacke asked the commander: "So, shall I do the rowing? [handle the takeoff]"

---

* There was no regulation requiring the crew to use the intercom. As a result the area microphone provided the only record of their conversation. Much of this was distorted and inaudible due to noise and the distance of the crew members from the microphone. The transcript, on which this account is based, nevertheless formed part of the official East African Community report.

Captain Krack replied, "Yes, please."

The aircraft turned left out of taxiway C and began backtracking down the runway toward the stopway at the end where it would turn 180 degrees and begin its takeoff roll.

Sitting in the center section between the wings Hermann Hennecke decided to change to a window seat for the takeoff. I might see something of Nairobi and the National Park, he thought, looking to his right, where there were empty seats.

He got up, still holding his paperback novel, and crossed the aisle to a seat right up next to the window and sat down. He had left all his other belongings behind on his center row seat. But he would only be gone a few minutes and would move back after takeoff; nothing would happen to his things in that short time.

Hennecke took up the end of the seat belt, slipped it through the grip, and pulled it very tight — an unusual action for him. Usually when he flew he simply hooked the belt up loosely because the airline insisted on you wearing one, but today he wore it tightly against his stomach.

He glanced up toward the nose, saw the stewardess settling herself on her doorway seat only four rows ahead, and stared out the window. The jet taxied smoothly out of the service area. The engines and the starboard wing angled back and he could see the runway rolling slowly by beneath the jet. I should see everything from here, he thought.

Up front in the first class section it seemed to Bob Laburn that they were moving rather soon after the new crew had boarded. Usually there was a long delay out on the apron, but today everything seemed to happen quickly.

The jet taxied out and he heard a woman's voice over the public address system. All seat belts should be fastened, she told them, and there should be no smoking during the takeoff.

"We wish you a pleasant flight," she said.

And then there was only the muffled noise of the engines and the slight bobbing motion as the aircraft taxied out.

Flight Engineer Rudi Hahn sat facing the nose of the aircraft with his seat in the forward position and read off the taxiing checklist. The big jet trundled slowly down the runway toward its turning point, engines roaring.

"Checklist," he called out. "Brakes."

"Are checked."

"Flaps," Rudi Hahn called out.

A different voice, probably Captain Krack's, responded: "Ten ten," followed by another word which may have been "Green." Both the flight engineer and the commander were expected to respond but the voice recorder failed to pick up a response from Rudi Hahn.*

This was the vital check which should have revealed that the leading edge flaps were not extended. In making it, the flight engineer was required to check a set of double filament lights on the right side of the pilot's center instrument panel, and then check two rows of eight double bulb lights on the extreme right-hand side of the flight engineer's panel. The lights were arranged in pairs, one yellow and one green. What Flight Engineer Hahn was looking for was a green light on the pilot's panel and eight green lights on his own panel. This would mean that both the leading edge flaps were fully extended. If any of the green lights was unlit, or if a yellow light was burning, the flaps would not be correctly positioned and the takeoff should not be attempted.

"Flight controls," the flight engineer continued.

The answer was indistinct.

"Yaw dampers." There was a pause, then: "Checked."

"Flight instruments and annunciator panels," Rudi Hahn called out.

"No warnings," said Captain Krack.

"No warnings here," reported Copilot Schacke.

Flight Engineer Hahn read off a succession of items, pausing as he checked each and gave his response.

* This may have been due to the limitations of the recorder already mentioned. The crew members concerned believed they had seen the correct number of leading edge green lights. The possibility of an electrical malfunction was considered by the East African Community investigators and, following technical evidence, was rejected.

"APU.

"Off. Door closed.

"Fuel temperature and heater.

"Checked and closed.

"Fuel panel and pressure.

"Checked. Pumps on.

"Cabin report.

"Not yet.

"Cockpit door is open.

"Stabilizer and trim."

Captain Krack made an incomprehensible comment.

"Stabilizer trim," First Officer Schacke reported and the rest was drowned by noise.

"Good."

"Yes."

"Rudder and aileron trim," Flight Engineer Hahn called out.

"Zero here, zero there," Copilot Schacke reported.

"Yes," confirmed Captain Krack.

"Yes," the flight engineer agreed. "Takeoff data."

"Yes," the copilot said and began to read off a series of numerical values which the recorder had difficulty in picking up, while in the background Flight Engineer Hahn could be heard talking to Purser Heidi Tischer.

Captain Krack called out: "Cabin report received."

"Checklist completed," Flight Engineer Hahn reported.

The jet had reached the end of the runway and Captain Krack began the turn into the stopway. At 7.51 A.M. the Control Tower broke in: "Lufthansa five four zero, your clearance."

"Go ahead," Copilot Schacke said.

"ATC clears Lufthansa five four zero Nairobi to Jan Smuts delta amber one zero," the Tower advised. "Climb and maintain flight level three five zero to Mike Bravo Mbeya echo departure and check clearance expires at five six. Time now is five one."

Back in the economy class compartment British businessman Terry Partridge from Sheffield came to the end of the last page of the book he had been reading, closed the book and placed it in the seat pocket in front of him. It was nicely timed. The jumbo was making its turn at the head of the runway and he shifted so he could watch the takeoff through the window, one seat away to his right.

He was sitting almost exactly halfway down the huge jet. There was only one row of seats behind him and then came the midway gap for the door that led out over the wing. He felt comfortable and relaxed. The flight so far had been smooth and trouble-free and for a man who averaged a hundred to a hundred and fifty flights a year it seemed to be just another ordinary trip. Like setting off in a car or bus.

He stared out and had that familiar sensation of the world outside wheeling slowly around as the jet turned in the stopway, lining up for the takeoff roll.

Captain Krack had completed the turn and *Hessen* faced south down runway 24. "We are ready to go," he said.

"So, let us do the check," Copilot Schacke called out.

Flight Engineer Hahn began reading the takeoff checklist: "So, landing lights."

"Normal, on," responded Captain Krack.

At 7.52½ A.M. the Control Tower interrupted: "Lufthansa five four zero cleared for takeoff. Surface wind calm."

"Transponder," Rudi Hahn challenged.

"Roger," one of the pilots answered the Control Tower. "Cleared for takeoff."

"Transponder," Rudi Hahn repeated.

"We don't have one," the copilot replied.

"Pack valves closed. Ignition is on. Body gear steering."

"Disarmed," said Captain Krack.

"Takeoff checklist is completed," Flight Engineer Hahn reported.

"Okay," Copilot Schacke acknowledged. He spoke briefly with the commander but there was too much noise; the recorder was overwhelmed. Captain Krack partially opened the throttles, Copilot Schacke took control of the nosewheel steering and the noise level rose as the roll began.

Behind them, Rudi Hahn adjusted the throttles to the correct −3A takeoff power. *Hessen*'s tires were spinning over the asphalt as the speed built up. The seconds ticked by, ten, fifteen, twenty . . . .

Twenty-four seconds after the roll had started Copilot Schacke called out: "Eighty."

Captain Krack started to speak, "Yes —" but the rest of his speech was drowned by noise.

Hessen's indicated airspeed was touching 80 knots and Rudi Hahn gave over control of the throttles to Captain Krack, but remained sitting forward so he could check the instruments on the pilot's center panel.

"Okay," the commander said.

The speed built up steadily, the takeoff run normal, thrust adequate and no evidence of excessive drag.

They were hurtling along the runway, approaching their target speed of 135 to 136 knots.

Thirty-eight seconds into the roll one of the pilots called out: "V1." (V1 is the point at which a plane reaches its takeoff speed and the pilot must decide whether or not to attempt the takeoff.)

In the next five seconds, shortly before *Hessen* reached its target rotation speed (VR), Copilot Schacke eased his forward pressure on the control column and began the rotation.

"VR," a voice called out.

The copilot began the rotation and *Hessen*'s nosewheel lifted smoothly about ten degrees from the runway. The aircraft's acceleration ended suddenly and for the next seven to eight seconds the jet rushed along nose up at about 145 knots. The wheels lifted somewhere between 2,500 and 3,000 yards down the runway and *Hessen* rose slowly into the air. As they were lifting, the three men in the cockpit saw birds flying past the nose.

Hessen climbed sluggishly away at about 450 feet a minute — far too slow. Normally they would have been climbing at 1,500 to 1,800 feet per minute and the airspeed would have been increasing dramatically as the jet surged out of "ground effect." But on this takeoff *Hessen*'s speed never got above 145 knots.

And then the aircraft began to shake.

Captain Krack called out: "Pay attention. Vibration —" his voice losing itself in the noise. He turned quickly to Rudi Hahn and asked him if there were any signs of abnormal engine vibration. The birds they had seen might have been sucked into the engines.

The flight engineer looked at his panel, checked the meters and warning lights and reported: "All is OK."

"Vibration," Captain Krack repeated, puzzled. Then he thought, it might be caused by unbalanced wheels. He checked the instruments, saw they indicated a positive rate of climb and started the retraction of the four large clusters of wheels and the nosewheel.

"Gear up," Copilot Schacke called and there was a metallic click as the lever went home and the cycle began. Flying along at 143 knots, *Hessen*'s landing gear doors began to open to receive the wheels, adding to the drag at a critical moment and cutting the airspeed by about 40 feet a minute. If the wheels could be lifted in time and the protruding doors closed, the aircraft's speed should increase by about 100 feet a minute. But this morning the undercarriage, which normally took about 21 seconds to raise, was still partly extended when *Hessen* struck the ground.

"Gear traveling," Copilot Schacke reported 18 seconds before impact.

Hessen had reached 100 feet above the ground and the rate of climb which had started out at between 400 and 500 feet a minute fell suddenly to zero. Copilot Schacke lost all feeling of acceleration and was forced to lower the nose to prevent the airspeed from dropping below 140 knots. The 747 began sinking gradually toward the earth.

"Engines okay so far," Flight Engineer Hahn called out.

Captain Krack acknowledged.

Six seconds passed.

"RPM is also okay," Flight Engineer Hahn informed the commander.

There was a harsh rattle as the control column shook, warning the crew of an approaching stall.

"Stickshaker," the flight engineer called out.

The automatic warning system rattled on for three seconds as *Hessen*'s speed fell dangerously to 140 knots. Captain Krack quickly placed his hands on the control column to lower the nose, but they were too close to the ground. There was no room to maneuver out of this desperate situation.

"Okay, crash!" Copilot Schacke broke in.

Through their headphones they could hear the Control Tower trying to summon the firefighting crews: "Fire Station Tower!"

The stickshaker rattled again.

"Fire Station Tower!"

The ground came up to meet them. In the last second Copilot Schacke closed all four throttles and the automatic warning horn designed to prevent flying crews from landing with their wheels up began to sound.

"Fire Station Tower!"

A SMALL FRENCH car carrying three passengers and a load of baggage turned off the Nairobi–Mombasa road and headed for Nairobi's Embakasi Airport. Jock Leslie-Melville, manager of a Nairobi-based photographic safari company, was taking his stepdaughter Dancy Bruce and her friend Esther Burton to catch a charter flight to London where Dancy worked for an antique dealer. They had been told to check in at eight but, knowing what charter flights could be like, they had planned to get there fifteen minutes early. So now they drove steadily along the road, tires swishing through puddles of overnight rain, windows rolled up to keep out the chill of the morning air. The clouds were thinning and way ahead down the airport road they could see the sun playing on the terminal building. Beyond the blurred yellow-brown grass, about four hundred yards to their right stretched the black ribbon of runway.

Dancy, sitting up front next to Jock, stared out at the passing African bush and knew deep down that after a few weeks in London she was going to be homesick for all this: the waving grass, broad plains and hugeness of the sky, the vast openness and space that was Africa. But she was looking forward to being back again in the whirl and tumult of big city London.

In a few hours she would be walking down London's streets. But until she arrived she would pay heavily in nervous tension; Dancy hated flying. Already that familiar ball of knotted nerves was throbbing down in her stomach and her mouth felt a little dry. But this time, at least, she would have the company of Esther Burton to while away the hours, friendly Esther who, before this morning, had not even seen a jumbo jet but had a secret ambition to fly in one.

And then as they rolled along the road, Dancy saw a jumbo jet hanging in the air above the runway, nose aimed upward, the sun reflecting off the tail, and she called out: "Look over there, Esther. That's your 747."

Esther sat up and looked out. Jock turned his eyes from the road to watch. The huge jet seemed to be heading directly toward them, coming slowly on in a peculiar nose-up, tail-down position.

"But what's it doing?" Esther asked.

"It must be landing —"

"It can't be," Jock said. "It's already past the runway."

Jock and Dancy stared at the jet and realized that something was wrong: it wasn't climbing any higher. It was flying along, almost level with them. Jock swung the car off the road and stopped almost without noticing what he was doing.

"It's crashing," Dancy said but she didn't, couldn't believe it. It flashed through her mind, maybe they've forgotten a passenger, or they're having some sort of trouble and they're turning back. It can't really crash.

The jumbo came drifting, floating slowly down, down, down. No sounds, no noise filtered through the rolled-up car windows. It was like a silent movie. The plane went toward the muddy earth, a giant modern airliner shining in the morning sun. At the last moment it dropped below the horizon. A split second later there was a flash. Brilliant flames shot up toward the sky. A great expanding fireball rose high over the bush and huge clouds of gray and dense black smoke billowed into the blue. The smoke twisted into a towering mushroom, Hiroshima-like, swirling and turning.

"Oh, God," Esther said.

Dancy turned away. She felt ill. All those people. Nobody would get out of a thing like that.

There was a silence in the car. They just sat there, the three of them, shocked, while the pall rose higher and higher above the bush.

The watchroom attendant at the Airport Fire Brigade tower watched, horrified, as the big jet appeared to falter in the air beyond the end of runway 24. The fire officer reached out and sounded the alarm bell. He heard it ringing harshly as he watched the plane, nose-up, dropping steadily toward the ground as it struggled ahead.

The duty crew grabbed their helmets and held tight as the fire tenders swung out, motors roaring, onto the runway. The sirens were screaming as they raced on behind the aircraft which was still flying but falling lower and lower all the time. The tail brushed some low bushes and struck the ground, scraping along for about a hundred yards. There was a flash of flame as *Hessen* rode up the embanked earth road. The engines on the left wing tore into the earthwork, pieces flying off, and the plane hurtled on over the top. Shattered by the impact, the tail section and the rear fuselage broke off behind the wings and began to disintegrate, hurling out passengers and crew. Fire flared up.

The forward section bounced into the air, shedding engines and an outer section of the left wing, came crashing back down and skidded 350 yards over the muddy earth, left wing blazing, then swung almost 180 degrees and plowed back toward the embankment. Thick mud slowed and then stopped the headlong thrust. *Hessen* came to rest leaned over to the left, the rear section behind the wings missing, the front section below the cockpit twisted and cracked.

The oncoming firemen saw dark oily smoke shooting skyward on the far side of the embankment. The fire engines began to brake and swing sharply to the west. The vehicles would never get over the eight-foot embankment. They headed for an emergency fire breakout road that would bring them out close to the wreckage. Sirens screaming, they roared along it and then they began to encounter the traffic of hundreds of sightseers.

Riding in one fire engine was Lufthansa's security man Norbert Diekmann. He had been on duty in the service area during the refueling stop and had turned to watch the 747's takeoff roll, fascinated even after all this time that an aircraft so huge could lift itself off the ground.

He had watched it thundering down the runway, seen the nosewheel lift and the jet rise slowly into the air until it was about 100 feet above the ground. And then he and the refueling crew had watched, shocked, as it came back to earth, still moving forward, nose up.

There was a flash as the plane smacked into the embankment and Diekmann heard a blast followed by another as the jet lurched over the top. Then he ran blindly, his hat under his arm.

As Diekmann raced toward the burning jumbo his heart froze. All his friends were aboard that plane and he wondered if he would ever see any of them again.

Back on the airfield, the Control Tower's urgent calls of "Fire Station Tower" had gone unanswered.

Suddenly there was a torrent of unintelligible words from one of the Fire Brigade vehicles. The Control Tower could only make out the words "aircraft," more noises, and "fire."

Then came a voice from the Fire Station: "Ah, Tower . . . Fire Station."

"Station, go ahead," the Tower instructed.

"Up till now there has not been any outside aid . . . the jumbo Lufthansa is . . . on fire," the Fire Station reported.

"Roger," the Control Tower acknowledged. "One five seven on board. One five seven."

Three and a half minutes after the jet had smashed into the road the Fire Station called the Control Tower again: "Would you inform the Airport Authority to come and assist the fire."

"Will you say again please, Fire Station," the Tower instructed.

VICTIMS

(*above*) Helmut Frankenburg. (*below*) Alfred and Veronika Solibakke

(*above*) Marie Galitzine, Unitours party leader. (*below*) Helge Nachtsheim, the 'Mickey Mouse' stewardess, and her husband Klaus

"Will you assist the . . . the . . . the fire people to the . . . to the incident of the accident just at the . . . " the words ran together, " . . . zero six."

"Fire Station, from Tower you are unreadable. Would you please say again slowly."

"I say again. The jumbo jet is on fire and up to now there's been no outside aid."

"Roger. Roger." Control Tower said. "We are doing it right now."

"Exchange seems to be asleep," the Fire Station commented.

"Roger."

The Fire Station broke in: "If you can get hold of the Ministry of Works yard, will you inform them to despatch some of their lorries to come and take the crews out to the incident of the accident."

"Roger. Will do that."

The Tower tried to contact the Fire Brigade vehicles speeding to the accident. "Fire Seven, confirm you are at the scene of the fire."

The Fire Station replied: "Affirmative." Because of the crowds, traffic and difficult terrain it took them almost five minutes to get there.

One of the vehicles answered. "Control Tower, this is Fire One. Do you read?"

"Fire One, go ahead."

"Will you ask the City Fire Brigade and Kenya Air Force for additional fire appliances bringing water, bringing water."

"Roger. Will do."

The voice came again: "Nairobi Tower, Fire One."

"Fire One, go ahead."

"Would you please immediately contact outside aids, outside aids. Over."

"We just asked for them," the Tower reported.

There was a jumble of words and a voice from Fire One at the scene of the wreck pleaded: "Send them immediately because the scene is horrible."

Takeoff and Impact

THE ROLL HAD STARTED almost immediately. There was no long wait at the head of the runway, no revving of engines. The big jet completed its turn and off it went. The engines were thrusting us along over ridges and bumps in the runway and the grass out left was beginning to blur. I felt uneasy, it seemed like we were moving too slowly and we'd never make it.

I looked right, past Lynn, past the rows and rows of seats and saw the airport buildings drawing level and I felt through the seat with my whole body every bump, jump, leap and lurch as we rocketed down the runway. Then I thought, stop it, stop panicking. It always feels too slow, and you always make it.

I looked left again, saw the wildly rushing grass, the whole world going madly by and thought, see, we're going fast enough. We'll make it.

Hermann Hennecke felt the jumbo rolling, rolling, rolling. First, he felt the thrust of acceleration and then he had a feeling the speed had fallen. The 747 wasn't going fast enough for takeoff.

My God, he thought as the jet thundered on, we must be nearing the end of the runway and we haven't taken off yet!

Tom Scott, sitting strapped in next to Jürgen Freund, could see the ground hurtling away behind them as the speed built up and felt himself bowing slightly with the acceleration. He had flown many hours as a pilot in the United States and knew all about takeoffs and aerodynamics, and so far he was happy. Everything seemed to be going along smoothly. He estimated they would soon be coming up to the pilot's velocity rotation point, the point at which the speed is just right and the pilot pulls back on the wheel, swings up the elevators in the tail, causing the tail to press down and the nosewheel to lift up off the runway.

There it was. The lift. Now after three or four seconds, when the angle was right, the jumbo should rise steadily and smoothly into the air, climbing solidly away with a thrust that would press the passengers back against their seats.

But in that instant after rotation Tom Scott felt something odd. The wheels bounced. A short sharp bounce. He had never felt that before and thought, that's strange, something's just not right. They weren't climbing as they should have been.

Ah, Hermann Hennecke thought, I was wrong. The jumbo has enough power after all. The pilot's made it, we're off the ground, and everything's fine.

He reached out, still strapped in, for his detective novel and in that moment everything began to shake. Things leaped up and jumped about. It sounded as if the whole aircraft was breaking up. He looked out and saw the wingtip swinging in a huge arc.

A few rows away, American sisters Tillie Harmel and Gladys Golman clasped hands across the aisle as they always did when flying together. They could see the skyline changing as the jet rose slowly.

"Beautiful," Tillie Harmel said.

Her sister agreed.

The angle of the skyline changed abruptly and the aircraft shuddered. Something was terribly wrong with the machine. The sisters looked at each other in alarm and their clasp tightened.

When the jumbo began to shudder violently, we knew we were

flying in a doomed aircraft. The engines were shaking in their mountings on the wings and there was a horrifying metallic coughing. I looked across at Lynn and thought, *this is it*.

Lynn grabbed at a glass of orange juice standing on the seat tray next to her. She caught the jumping glass, but the juice leaped up over her hair.

The jumbo was still struggling to get up and away from the runway, but there was none of that thrusting power we had felt in Frankfurt. We were up about a hundred feet and looking down I saw that the ground was staying the same distance away.

Tom Scott looked out the window to see the wing jerking wildly and condensation streaming over the top. He couldn't understand it, there was no reason for the shaking. There was no wind, and they were still so low they should have been protected from any gusts. And that condensation — it shouldn't be that wet out there over the wings.

In the fractions of seconds it took to notice this, Scott realized the plane was stalling. He couldn't believe it. With all the precautions the airline took and with all the built-in safety devices aboard the 747, how could it possibly happen?

After twenty seconds of flight as the jumbo continued to shudder through the air he thought, we're too low. Far, far too low. We're about a hundred feet off the ground. At this point we should be at least a thousand feet up and climbing.

Then he knew they would crash. They would come hurtling back down and he knew from statistics that he wouldn't survive, that few people had ever survived stall incidents on takeoff at such a low altitude. They would plow back into the earth and all of them would be killed.

Thoughts raced through his mind, spurred by the realization that everything would soon be blotted out, that his life was nearly over. Why, he thought, why do I have to be on this plane? I wish I was sitting up in that cockpit. At least I wish I knew what's causing that stall. What is happening up there? Do they know?

Beyond the windows he could see the wing was still shaking.

They were coming down. Tom Scott leaned his head back and closed his eyes and thought about his family, what they would have to go through because of this, how his wife Alexandra back home in Bad Soden would feel when they told her. He didn't want to see the end. He kept his eyes shut tight and gripped tightly on the seat. Any second now. He wondered what it would feel like to hit the ground, if he would live through the impact, if it would be a slow death.

"We're not gaining altitude fast enough," Karl Kahn yelled to his daughter Nancy. He did a lot of flying on business in the United States but this takeoff was unlike anything he had ever experienced — shaking and shuddering and a frightening lack of thrust.

Nancy nudged him. "That looks like smoke."

He looked out and to him it seemed like low hanging cloud. The jumbo passed through it.

"Cloud," he said loudly.

Hermann Hennecke stared in disbelief out at the muddy earth. The big jet couldn't be coming down. They would pull out of it, they had to. They would pull out of it and this terrible shaking would stop. Then he saw the ground coming up and he knew suddenly that they wouldn't.

"We're coming down," Karl Kahn shouted.

Nancy Kahn whipped off her glasses and thrust them into the seat pocket in front of her. It was instinctive: *get them off your face.* She yelled out to those around her: "Take off your glasses!"

She put her head on her knees and waited for it.

"This is the end," John Bing thought as the shaking worsened. Loose objects were flying about the cabin, lockers were snapping open, blankets, briefcases and packages came tumbling down.

"Let it be painless," he said to himself. "Please let it be painless."

Up in the nose, Bob Laburn felt the jumbo shuddering. The

man next to him put his head on his knees. Bob glanced quickly at him and did the same. The emergency instructions, he thought, but who ever remembers?

A few seats away Malcolm Solts felt the jumbo losing all power and sensed something awful was going to happen. They were being hurled forward and back, only the seat belts keeping them in their seats. He reached up, snatched his glasses off his face, threw them on the floor, and rolled himself up with his head on his knees.

We had passed the end of the runway. Now, below us, was only rough bush. The jumbo began to lose height, still nose-up. We were going in — the fears of a lifetime had become a reality — but my mind still refused to accept it. No, I argued desperately, we *can't* crash, I don't want us to crash. We've got our whole lives ahead of us, there's still so much I want to do, and those two sons of ours . . . why did I bring them with me?

I stared out of the window, anguished, unable to react, sensing death ahead and feeling icy cold in my back — helpless. The ground came closer.

"Put your head down!" my wife shouted and I pulled Garett down so his head was on his knees. Brendon was still sleeping, sprawled back in his seat. I tried, but couldn't reach him. It was unearthly inside the jet. No one screamed. No one shouted to us to do anything. There was only that mechanical coughing, the sound of things crashing about, objects falling. Some passengers were still sitting erect in their seats.

Garett lifted his head to look.

"Stay down!" I shouted, pushing at him.

I saw the nun in the row ahead bow her head. I ducked.

Alarmed, Elinor Senkler tapped her husband's shoulder and asked: "Are we in trouble?"

Former Royal Canadian Air Force pilot Edmund Senkler stared out of his port side window and saw the engines shaking on the wing. This is a prestall flutter, he realized. How is our pilot going to stop us from going into a spin? His wartime training came back to him: pull back on the throttles, drop the nose.

He felt *Hessen*'s nose had dropped and felt relieved. We'll glide in for an emergency landing in this flat field, come to a stop and climb out.

The jet sank lower and lower. Out of nowhere, an embanked earth road loomed up. Senkler saw they were heading straight for it.

At the last moment Steward Tom Scott felt the engines throttling back to idle and thought, oh great, the captain's found a field or some place to set the plane down. We might just get out of this after all.

On the other side of the cabin, Hermann Hennecke stretched his arms out in front of him and dropped his head. There was a sickening crash as some part of the machine struck. He was hurled against his seat belt. There were no screams, no shouts, nothing, as the Boeing bounced across the earth, seats breaking loose, luggage coming down from the overhead lockers. And then the lights went out.

Margaret Hooker and Carol Mall had been chatting during the takeoff. As the nose lifted, Carol put her hand up to her face and took off her glasses. At the same time Margaret remembered her husband telling her he'd seen animals on the ground once while taking off from Nairobi, and she'd turned her head thinking, I'll look and see if I can see any. She was so intent on the bush she didn't notice the earth rapidly coming closer.

There was a flash and they were scraping the ground. It was so quick, like being in the center of an explosion, a tremendous concussion, and Margaret felt she was somersaulting. She and the seat and Carol were going through the air together. An unbelievable sensation. Unreal. They crashed down through the floor but she felt no pain, nothing at all. The jumbo had cracked open and they were dropping through into the dark of the baggage hold below.

Edmund Senkler, still sitting up and staring out of the window felt a jarring blow hit his back and was thrown forward as the tail slammed into the ground in front of the road. The jumbo reared up, bouncing over the embankment. He saw sparks flying past the window and heard metal tearing somewhere behind. Pieces of plastic from the roof hurtled past his head. And then the jet struck again.

Passengers in the first class compartments heard a wrenching sound. Bob Laburn lifted his head to see what had happened and everything went black.

My head smashed into the seat in front of me. The rows of seats came loose from the floor and folded forward like a pack of cards. We were crushed in between. I was looking to my left and saw Brendon being hurled like a rag doll.

I shouted: "Are you all right, are you all right?"

He didn't answer and I thought, my God, his neck's broken.

Then we jerked again. I felt like we were on the ground and sliding along. The aircraft slowed to the left. There were ripping sounds and sections of the roof, lockers and luggage began falling on us. Dust filled the cabin.

I saw a fireball of flame erupting where the port wing had been. Right next to us it was all flames and thick black smoke. I realized that there was only a small sheet of glass between Brendon and the blaze.

The first impact drove Tom Scott back hard against his seat but it was only a glancing blow. The jumbo struck again and this one really shook him up — he felt it in his back. He opened his eyes and saw they were sliding along, riding over the rough ground, the aircraft lurching and groaning as it broke up. Amazed that nothing was happening to him, he sat holding on, waiting as they slid.

On the starboard side of the economy cabin a cupboard housing the crew's serving trolleys burst open. Passengers near the aisle saw the trolleys go speeding toward Stewardess Antje Kollner who was sitting alone at her position near the door over the wing.

The young blond stewardess leaped out of her seat and jumped aside. The trolleys smashed into the seat she had just left. Moments later, the ceiling shattered and an inflatable dinghy pack fell heavily, blocking the doorway, but missing the stewardess by inches.

The luggage lockers above Terry Partridge's head broke off the ceiling and came tumbling down. He raised his arm to fend off a dark object and his briefcase and jacket fell down onto him. That damned locker. He'd had trouble earlier keeping it shut. Now it had almost killed him.

The jumbo bounced over the bush and Terry Partridge looked to his left. Beyond the rows of seats and windows he saw something that filled him with dread. The port wing was rubbing on the ground and all along it flames were shooting up. The jumbo was on fire!

As the aircraft slowed, the force was tremendous. John Bing saw debris and loose overhead luggage change direction and fall back on top of the cowering people. Some of them were struck on the head.

He was alarmed, looked across the aisle at his wife Jean. Was she all right? He saw her sitting there, three places away, gripping the seat. A huge section broke off the ceiling and swung down. He watched, horrified, as it fell and struck his wife in the chest. It must have killed her, he thought, anguished.

Malcolm Solts held on tightly, the impact hurling him heavily against his seat belt. He heard glass breaking and metal tearing and crumpling. The inside of the jet seemed to be coming apart. Panels shattered, jagged sheets of plastic flew everywhere. There were bumps and groaning noises as the jet plowed on. He kept his head down against his knees. Hold on, he told himself. Keep holding on.

The floor jarred and heaved and rocked beneath his feet. Things fell on him, baggage, dust, chunks of ceiling, but he held doggedly on, shoulders hunched, head down, as the plane broke up.

When the long jarring slide ended abruptly, Tom Scott couldn't believe he was still alive. To his left everything was shattered and broken and to his right, there were flames. Fire leaped up outside the door. Angrily he thought, oh boy, here you've survived the crash and now you'll burn to death because you can't get out.

"Wake up, it's a crash!"

HANS NEEB WAS BADLY shaken, but he was alive. In the quiet compartment forward of the wings he raised his head from between his arms. The jumbo had stopped moving and he wasn't even hurt. At impact the seats in front of him had broken off the floor and crashed toward the first class compartment. Dust and splintered plastic were still showering down on him where he sat strapped to his seat.

He looked about, listened for voices, cries for help, but there weren't any. The silence after the noise of the impact was unnerving. He knew he had to get up and out — right away.

He loosened his seat belt and stood up, his eyes taking in the wreckage of the cabin as he stepped out into the aisle. Remembering there was a door somewhere to his right a few rows from his seat, he moved quickly toward it, shouting: *"Raus! Raus!"* He didn't think about his baggage — just that door and getting out.

At the doorway Neeb saw a stewardess pushing and struggling to get the door open. It seemed to have jammed.

After the movement stopped Hermann Hennecke heard no sound from the other passengers. Then a voice shouted: "We must get out!"

Confused in the half-dark, unable to think logically or understand what had happened, Hermann peered back at his old seat over in the center section but couldn't see any of the other passengers who had been there only seconds before. Where were they? What had happened to them?

And then he saw small tongues of flame flickering across the collapsed ceiling edges near the back.

Hermann tugged at his seat belt and felt it unclasp in his hands. Four rows ahead he picked out the bright yellow uniform of a stewardess at the exit door. She had both hands on the door handle and was pulling desperately at it, trying to get it to move. It had to turn more than 180 degrees.

Will she do it, he thought, paralyzed in his seat, eyes on the woman. She must get it open. She must. We'll all die in the fire.

On the other side of the aircraft, Steward Tom Scott was still sitting in his crew seat, struggling to control his anger.

Finally his emergency evacuation training took over and he unbuckled his seat belt and jumped up. He had to try and get all these people out. There was no way out this side, they would all go straight into the fire. Try the other side.

He ran at the wreckage of the kitchen, fighting, punching his way through the shattered ceiling panels and toppled equipment. He saw movement ahead of him at the starboard door — Stewardess Evelyn Rehm and a passenger were battling to get the door open.

As Scott joined them in the doorway he saw they had managed to get the door partly open. Together they all pushed and pushed. The door swung back against the fuselage and daylight streamed in.

One moment Hermann Hennecke was sitting fixed in his seat, then he was right next to the door. He didn't know how he had got there, but he found himself jumping, not through a door, it seemed, but into the light. First he was falling, then he hit the ground and toppled forward onto his hands. There was no pain, only a feeling of relief. He started to crawl away out of the mud on his hands and knees, the first person out of the economy section.

As he was crawling something struck him on the back. It's the side of the plane, Hermann thought. It's burst open and I'm under it. He didn't stop to look, but scrambled frantically out from underneath the huge object, got shakily to his feet and stumbled off, half running, over the rough ground with only the open air before him.* He was repeating crazily to himself, "You are out! You are out!"

He was still running, everything ahead a little hazy and strange, when there was an explosion behind him. He turned to look at the burning jet and realized suddenly why things looked so odd: he had lost his glasses. But he still saw the flames, great fuzzy flames, leaping up over the wreck from which he had escaped.

The escape chute inflated, and, intact and undamaged, bridged the gap between the door and the ground. Everything looked perfect for escape and Tom Scott's instincts screamed at him, run, get out of here as fast as you can. Then he told himself, you can't do that, you've got to stay. You're a trained person and you've got to help all these people out.

Most of the passengers were still sitting dazed in their seats. Some had even stood up and taken off their coats. He turned and started to shout in a mixture of German and English: "*Raus!* Out! *Raus!* Out!" He was amazed at the power of his voice. It didn't seem like it belonged to him, yelling out hoarsely, urgently in the crumbling wreckage.

The passengers came alive. They jumped up, came running bunched together, scared and wide-eyed toward the door. He grabbed them as they came, grabbed arms, shoulders, collars, jackets, shirt sleeves and hurled them down the chute. He wasn't too gentle, but he didn't want any blockages in the doorway now and, anyway, a broken leg was better than burning in a plane. Out, out, out they went, landing on their bottoms, some on their

---

* Airline officials later suggested he had been hit by the escape chute as it inflated.

sides, scrambling the rest of the way with their hands and feet. There was no panic, no screaming, but there was fear. A woman fell down a few yards in front of the doorway and the passengers coming on behind ran right over her.

Two rows from the door, Renate Kahn froze in her seat. All she could think was don't move, stay put until someone gives you some sort of instructions. She sat watching the drama at the door, and heard Tom Scott shouting, "*Raus!* Out!"

Then she responded to his command and her whole attention was focused on that door. She didn't think to look back and see what had happened to Karl and Nancy sitting a few rows behind, but jumped up and ran, reached the door and was pushed down the chute. Halfway down, she got stuck because the angle was not steep enough. She got herself moving with her hands and legs, stepped off into the mud and stood rooted to the ground at the bottom of the chute, watching for her family to appear in the doorway above. In her dazed state it did not occur to her that the jumbo she was standing next to was only seconds away from exploding.

Back in the jumbo Karl and Nancy Kahn had seen her go. Karl threw down his camera, grabbed his daughter's arm and shouted: "Let's get out!"

Parts of the ceiling were coming down on them. Nancy snatched her glasses from the seat pocket, leaped up and ran for the door in her heavy hiking boots. Karl was right with her and they went together through the door onto the chute, slid as far as they could, got up and ran off to find Renate standing looking at them.

"Run. It's going to explode!" Karl shouted and they took off over the bush.

Behind the Kahns came the American sisters Tillie Harmel and Gladys Golman. They were on the chute when Karl Kahn shouted and it scared them. If the jumbo blew up now . . .

Halfway down Tillie Harmel lost a shoe. She hesitated, leaned back for it, couldn't reach it, and her sister slid past her to the ground.

Gladys Golman leaped up, grabbed Tillie's leg and pulled her down the slide. Tillie got up and the sisters ran together through the mud, Tillie struggling along in one shoe.

Ahead, Karl Kahn yelled: "Keep going, keep going. It's going to explode!"

Tillie Harmel stopped, took off her remaining shoe and ran on, holding it in her hand. She was breathing harshly, mouth open from exertion, but kept on running. She was exhausted — badly shocked — and it was a long time before she realized she had been injured.

John Bing looked through the window on his left and was horrified. The wing out there was ablaze, the flames so close he could feel the heat. Get out of here, his instincts shouted at him. Get away from the fire. He was unstrapped in seconds, jumped up and rushed across the aisle to his wife afraid he might find her dead.

Jean Bing was sitting surrounded by wreckage from the ceiling. John grabbed at it and was surprised by its lightness. Jean was moving; she seemed unhurt. Thank God she was all right.

A woman's voice was shouting: "This way! Out here!"

The voice came from the far side of the jumbo and the Bings went toward the sound away from the fire. They crossed the broken-up cabin awkwardly, feet crunching over debris on the floor, dust and wreckage still tumbling down. Ahead they saw the yellow uniform of a stewardess. There was wreckage blocking the doorway and the young woman was bent down, hurling it aside. The way was clear. She tugged at the handle and the door over the wing swung outward. There were now two doors open for the survivors to use.

"Out of here!" she shouted and started pushing the passengers through.

People were crowded together near the door and lined up behind the Bings, but everyone was moving quickly now. The Bings went through the doorway together and found themselves walking on a half-inflated escape chute over the top of the wing. But no one needed it. The wing was resting right on the ground.

The Bings stepped quickly over the curved surface and hopped down off the rear edge flaps into the mud. Someone was shouting to them all to run, to get away from the jet, and the Bings ran, John in his shirtsleeves and Jean limping, one shoe missing.

Close behind came Terry Partridge, carrying his briefcase and his jacket as if he was getting off quite normally at an airport.

Elinor Senkler sat immobile. Everything, it seemed, had stopped. After the heavy noises of the impact and the groan of tearing metal, the sudden silence was eerie.

Then she thought, we're alive. We've survived.

She looked left. Edmund Senkler was moving, groping with his hand under the seat, and Elinor realized, he's feeling for the camera.

"Eddie, leave it," she screamed at him, pulling, tugging at her seat belt. "Get out, it's gonna blow!"

She felt the seat belt loosen and sprang up out into the aisle. Which way out? Edmund brushed past, ran for the exit door a few rows behind their seats and grabbed the handle that would swing it open.

He had both hands on the handle, was starting to pull, and he saw fire. The wing outside was ablaze.

"No," a stewardess yelled across at him. "This way, this way!"

Edmund started to say something about the fire.

"No," she shouted back at him. "This side."

Elinor heard the stewardess shouting and stumbled in her direction through the four-seat center section, tramping over camera cases and purses and bags that lay on the floor. She held onto the head rests to steady herself, moving quickly between the seats, slipping and scrambling. She came out into the far aisle and saw the exit door ahead and the stewardess shoving passengers through into the daylight.

And Edmund was right behind her. He had run through between the toilet cabinets. They leaped through the door and ran over the wing to the ground. Ahead, Elinor saw a man running away.

"It's going to blow," she yelled and they struggled out of the mud and started to run.

Hans Neeb had been helping in the forward doorway. When he left the plane, he found himself walking, half-running down the chute to the ground. He looked around as he touched the earth, saw smoke and flame coming from the far side of the wreckage and told himselt to run, knowing the plane would explode.

After he had run a short distance he stopped and looked back. People were leaping down from the door he had just left and others were coming down a chute over the right wing. The rear section behind the wings was completely gone. The tail had completely disintegrated; there were huge cracks in the front section and the left side was covered in flames. A voice was calling for help and Neeb saw an elderly man struggling nearby. He went up to him, got an arm under the man, supporting him with his shoulders, and walked him slowly away. When they had gone some distance, he lowered the man gently to the ground. He would be safe here. What he needed now was an ambulance.

Explosions shook the burning jet. He saw people still coming out, the flames growing higher all the time, and coming toward him was the familiar face of his German colleague Dr. Gerd Kampf-Emden. He had no shoes on and blood was dripping from one of his feet. Hans Neeb ran over and they shook each other's hands.

"Ja," Dr. Kampf-Emden said grimly in German, "we have just escaped from the devil's shovel."

Mother Dietlende sat dazed in her seat. She did not know how long she had sat there staring ahead into the gloom. In those first few moments she did not realize the danger she was in. The jumbo was burning and it might explode at any second. She noticed her passport and purse lying on the floor next to her feet, unstrapped herself and bent down to pick them up. The bag they had fallen from was overturned. She righted it and packed the two items inside, working unhurriedly with her hands, oblivious to all that was happening around her.

When she stood up it hit her. She saw the wreckage and destruction inside the jumbo and she was all alone — no one else was in sight. She was desperately afraid. Turning toward the back of the jumbo to where the four Solanus sisters had been sitting, she could only see tangled wreckage. She thought she saw flames.

Bewildered, she tried to climb over the wreckage in the next aisle, praying desperately, "Lord God, if You still need me in the mission, then help me now when I need help."

The impact had left me stunned in my seat.

"Get out!" my wife screamed, "Get out!" She was struggling with her seat belt.

I unbuckled my belt and Garett's and dragged him out into the aisle. He moved without speaking, eyes wide, like a robot. I leaned over to pull up the armrests. We had to get Brendon out. The whole side of the plane was a sheet of flame licking right up against the glass of the windows. It crackled and roared as it burned. I thought, we'll never make it. We're going to be burned.

Lynn leaped across the aisle, came up from behind and unbuckled Brendon's belt, shouting: "Wake up, it's a crash! It's a crash!" and dragged him, mumbling, half-asleep, into the aisle.

"Is he all right?"

"Yes," Lynn cried, "yes!"

In the seat behind us I saw an old man with blood pouring from his forehead. He was making no effort to get out. He just sat there looking dazed, the blood spilling down. I didn't know whether to help him or not.

"Get out!" Lynn shouted to me, "Quickly!"

But there was debris all around. A huge section of ceiling blocked our path. The overhead lockers had fallen in. All sorts of stuff was raining down, white powdery material, chips of plastic, pieces of luggage. The whole jet was closing in on us, and all the time there were flickering flames at the windows and a smell that tore at the throat and nostrils.

Behind us, the rear section of the plane was missing. A diffused light filtered through the jagged wreckage and Lynn instinctively moved toward it seeking a way out. "No!" I shouted, "Go forward!" I had Garett's hand and pushed ahead. I managed, one-handed, to hurl aside the roofing, to smash through the wreckage, and head up toward the front. Someone was coming close behind us: the nun.

There was no escape to the left, only flames. I saw the safety diagram in my mind: we had to go up and right. Dragging Garett I got to the kitchen and pulled him into it. From the starboard side of the aircraft I heard a voice shouting hoarsely: "*Raus!* Out! *Raus!*"

The kitchen was in ruins and part of the equipment had fallen over, blocking our path. A man came up beside me and together we kicked — once, twice. The object broke up in fragments and we were through. The nun ran past.

Mother Dietlinde found herself sliding down the escape chute with her bag in her hand. Near the bottom she got stuck. She stood up, saw the muddy earth around her and felt faint. Everything went dark before her eyes and she felt she was falling.

Someone took her by the arm and she heard a man's voice say: "Quick, sister, we must get away from here."

She leaned gratefully on the man and was led away through the mud, passing through a nightmarish scene of bodies, injured people and wreckage that seemed to spread everywhere. She stumbled on, weak and dazed, and finally reached a mound in the field, sat down and bowed her head, deeply shocked.

I could see the open doorway ahead, daylight streaming in and people leaping out and down, when I lost my wife. I looked back desperately but still couldn't see her. My God, I thought, hesitating near that doorway flanked by two yelling crew members, what's happened to them? I didn't know what to do. Should I throw Garett down the chute and go back for them? Should we jump and leave them? Or should we both go back?

"Lynn," I shouted. "Where are you?"

She was coming through the wreckage, holding Brendon by the hand.

"Get out," she shouted. "We're all right. Get out!"

A dark-haired steward grabbed my arm shouting, "*Raus! Raus!*" and hurled me through the door and down the chute. Alongside came Garett, shoved by a stewardess. Behind came Lynn and Brendon, both in socks.

There was an explosion as we hit the ground, a hollow boom from the far side of the aircraft. A man shouted: "Run, it's going to explode! Run!"

We got up and ran through the mud. I was terrified that the fuel tanks would ignite and engulf us in a giant explosion. Ahead of us a man with a limp was running wildly across the bush, looking back, stumbling, regaining his balance and carrying on. Brendon had no shoes. I picked him up and ran with him over the rough ground. He seemed dazed, half asleep. When we had gone about fifty yards Garett tripped and fell face down. When he scrambled to his feet his face was covered in mud. My wife was crying: "My babies, oh my babies! Thank God you're safe. Thank God."

At the doorway forward of the wing, people were still arriving in twos and threes to be thrown down the chute. A woman slipped on broken eggs from the kitchen and fell heavily. Stewardess Evelyn Rehm leaned down to help her, lost her balance and tumbled out of the doorway onto the chute and landed in a heap on the muddy earth. Above her, Tom Scott was still pushing the people out, the last crew member still aboard the burning jet.

The jumbo was vibrating and shaking beneath him, smoke filling the interior, flames shooting up fiercely to the left. Finally there weren't any more passengers left. All those who could walk were out and Scott stood alone in the trembling jet. It's a time bomb, he thought, and it's going to explode at any second. He wanted to jump out and run, to get as far away as he could before the big explosion ripped everything apart. But he couldn't just leave without checking. He had to see if there was anyone still in the plane who was trapped, or unconscious, or who couldn't walk.

Tom Scott ran forward, looked left and right in the quiet compartment, saw nobody, turned back to take a last look in the non-smoking section between the wings, hoping desperately that it would be empty.

The jumbo was quivering; there were small explosions off to the left, and he wanted to get out of it right away. He took one last look to clear his conscience, peering through the murk and the dust and the smoke, and he saw someone still in there. An old man was sitting leaned over in his seat, way back on the left side of the nonsmoking area, blood dripping from a gash in his forehead.

Oh no, Tom despaired, oh no. A conflict raged in his mind: if I try to save him I'll never make it. He must weigh about 200 pounds. I'll never be able to get him out of here in time and heck, he's an old man, he's probably not going to be around much longer anyway. I've risked my life long enough in here, I should get out. I have a duty to my wife and my parents. I've risked enough.

These thoughts flashed through his mind in seconds — terrible thoughts — but he knew he'd have to try to save the old man. He couldn't leave him — if he did it would bother him for the rest of his life.

Tom Scott rushed up and grabbed the old man. He looked up, stunned, and asked the steward in German: "Where is my case?"

"Forget your case, grandpa," Tom yelled at him. "We've got to get out of here."

He reached down and dragged the old man out into the aisle. The flames were right up against the windows and there was the hissing and crackling of burning fuel. The jumbo was vibrating ominously. The whole thing was ready to explode. Tom Scott had his arm around the old man's body and was half-dragging him through the wreckage. Faster, faster. They didn't have much time.

He got him to the door, bent down and took the old man's weight over his shoulders. They went down the chute together and ran clumsily through the mud at the bottom. They stumbled off toward the other passengers they could see gathered about a hundred yards from the jumbo. When they reached them Tom

Scott saw the old man was clutching a dark attaché case. He'd saved it after all.

Margaret Hooker wasn't sure if she had been unconscious or if she had simply been sitting there, numbed, in her seat down in the baggage hold all the time. She couldn't remember clearly what had happened. She was now surrounded by metal. There was a board in front of her and she managed to place it: it had been in the first class compartment, a yard or two in front of them, before the takeoff began. The stewardesses had used it to hold trays and drinks while they were serving.

Right by her shoulder the fuselage had burst open. Through a great jagged hole she could see small flames flickering out on the ground and a man running toward the plane, leaping over rings of fire. He must have seen her, but he said nothing and she lost sight of him.

She loosened her seat belt and found she couldn't move. Her foot was caught in the wreckage. She felt no pain and there was no blood but why couldn't she get her foot out?

She pulled, gritted her teeth, jerked really hard, and tore her foot free. There was a deep ragged slash right through her foot but still no blood appeared and she couldn't feel anything.

She tried to get up but something pulled her back into the seat and puzzled, she looked down. Her slacks were snared on the bottom of the seat. She tugged at them, hoping they would tear free, but they wouldn't. She was still trapped in the jumbo.

There was only one thing to do. Margaret wriggled out of her slacks, thanking God for the elastic in the top, and stepped through the crack in the side of the aircraft in her underwear. She was standing on the ground in pools of kerosene and felt the coldness of her bare feet, but she was not afraid and she felt she was thinking very clearly. She reached back into the wreckage, unhooked her slacks and, surrounded by jet fuel with flames a short way off, stepped calmly back into her pants.

Margaret looked in through the crack and saw the row of seats hanging there about knee-high off the ground. And then she saw her friend Carol Mall lying sprawled back in her seat, eyes closed, blood oozing from small cuts on her eyebrows. Carol opened her eyes as Margaret looked at her.

"My God, Carol, what has happened?" Margaret cried out.

But Carol did not speak. She lay staring up at her companion and Margaret guessed she had been badly injured.

"Don't worry," she said, leaning in, "I won't leave you."

And, consoling her, she reached across and unfastened Carol's seat belt. Carol raised her arms but she still said nothing.

"I'll get you out of here, Carol, don't you worry."

Margaret got her arms under Carol and lifted her up, surprised at how light Carol was and how easy it was to move her. Talking softly, she drew the injured woman slowly through the torn metal and out of the crack. Margaret looked down and saw, right there on a seat, her handbag with her passport and money and things all spilled out. She told herself, grab your passport, it's a valuable document and you'll need it. She scooped it up in one hand, dropped it back in the bag and swung the bag up over her arm in a quick, instinctive action. She set off, hobbling along, bent under Carol Mall's weight, and stepping slowly through the puddles of fuel next to the fuselage.

For the first time Margaret became aware of other things: circles of flame on the ground, dark smoke rising into the sky from somewhere behind her and voices calling for help from the first class compartment. But there was nothing she could do for them. She staggered on past the nose and saw people standing some distance away.

"Hurry," they shouted to her. "It's going to explode!" But she couldn't move any faster. A group of people ran over and took Carol from her and ran with her away from the burning jet. They were not far away when *Hessen* exploded, the fire roaring skyward above the cabin they had just left and she thought, my God, all those people are still inside.

But no one could get near. The flames were too fierce.

I looked back and saw flames erupting high over the cabin. A pall of smoke swirled into the sky. Dust and muck was raining down on us. The tail section was missing and the nose was not there and people were running wildly away. With a shock, I noticed that the shattered jet had swiveled around and now lay facing back the way we had come. I called to Lynn, "The jet spun right round, d'you see that? We turned right round!" Lynn didn't understand, and merely sobbed out, "What?"

We ran on. I was shouting, "Keep going, keep going!" afraid parts of the jumbo might fly off. When we reached the top of the slope the skyline seemed to come alive. A large crowd of Kenyans was rushing toward the aircraft. Four of them, a woman and three men, came up to us and embraced us, shaking hands.

"You are safe," they said, wide-eyed, and stroked the children. "God is with you today!" I felt an overwhelming sense of comfort, like being a child again, being mothered, protected. After all the traveling, the death and sudden destruction, we had come back to the warm and tender arms of Africa.

A man offered us his broken shoes, pointing at Lynn's and Brendon's mud-covered socks. I felt close to tears.

(*above*) The *Hessen* cabin crew pictured the evening before the crash. (*below*) Firemen spray foam to put out the last of the blaze. (Marion Kaplan)

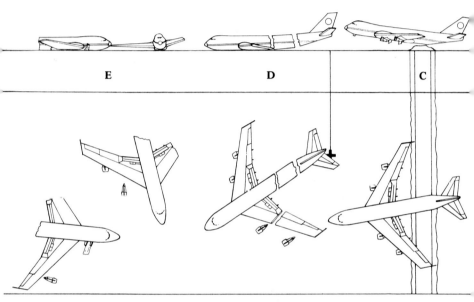

PLAN AND ELEVATION OF CRASH SEQUENCE

A. A few seconds after takeoff, *Hessen* had reached an altitude of 100 feet (30 m). Because the leading edge flaps were not extended, the jet began to stall and failed to gain height

B. *Hessen* fell in a nose-up position and hit the ground for the first time 370 feet (112 m) from the end of the runway

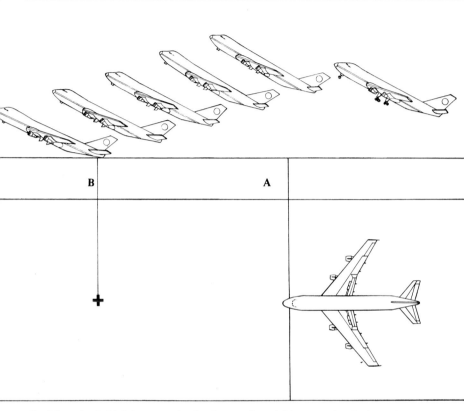

C. After the initial impact, the jet bounced and hit an embanked earth road. The tail began to break off
D. On the far side of the road, the tail and middle section disintegrated. A portion of the left wing broke off, shedding the two left engines
E. The remaining section of the jet pivoted in the mud and came to rest facing back toward the airport

Captain Christian Krack

Trapped

THERE WAS CHAOS in the first class compartment. Great cracks opened up in the floor, so deep they went right through to the ground, and the cabin twisted in the impact. The floor sloped at different angles, seats were torn off and sections of the staircase and the upstairs lounge broke loose and crashed down onto the passengers below.

Purser Heide Tischer, thirty-nine, and Stewardess Lydia Lux, twenty-five, were strapped into a twin-seat on the left side directly under the lounge when it came down. The floor collapsed and their seats pitched through into the baggage hold. They gripped hands. Heide Tischer cried out, "My God!" and Lydia Lux screamed.

As *Hessen*'s long slide ended Captain Krack reached out and pulled the four engine fire switches. He and Flight Engineer Hahn sprang onto their seats and reached for the overhead escape hatch. It wouldn't open. They pushed and punched at it but nothing happened. It was stuck tight.

The service hatch door, Flight Engineer Hahn thought. He jumped down and operated the lock on the door that was on the right-hand side of the cockpit, managing to get it open and wrench it inward. The door swung about five inches, then stopped. Rudi Hahn tried to force it, pulling with both hands, but the impact must have damaged the door and he couldn't get it to open any further. He could stick an arm or a leg out but that was all.

Copilot Schacke saw Krack and Hahn battling and realized that they would have to go through the cocktail bar and downstairs to the first class compartment. He pushed through to the top of the stairs and hesitated. The stairway was blocked by wreckage.

His fellow crew members joined him, prodded at the wreckage and saw it give. The whole thing might shatter under their weight.

"We'll have to go down there," the copilot said.

Rudi Hahn jumped. The wreckage broke under him and he fell right through, landing heavily on his back on the cabin floor below.

The two men called down to him, "Rudi, are you all right?"

Hahn sat up and got to his feet, clutching his right shoulder, his face twisted in agony. He could barely move his arm. Captain Krack came crashing down next bringing some wreckage tumbling after him, and shouting, "*Raus!* Out! Everybody out!"

Then Krack jumped into a gap in the floor and scrambled out of the cabin through a hole on the right of the fuselage. Behind him, Hahn went left and crawled through a hole in the port side. He stood up and was starting to stumble off awkwardly when two men he had never seen ran up, took him by the arm and led him away.

Back aboard *Hessen*, Heide Tischer and Lydia Lux found themselves trapped in a metal cavern. There was a narrow gap in front of Heide's right foot that funneled out into a large crack. Beyond that she could see the earth.

Heide freed herself from her seat and squeezed through the hole, her clothes tearing as they caught. Lydia Lux came on behind and together they crawled quickly through, stepped down and found themselves standing on the ground. Outside the wreck they were confronted with a wall of flames.

Heide quickly looked around her and saw a patch of earth to her right where the fire had not yet taken hold. The two women hesitated, then ran, passing between the flames and the wrecked cabin and coming out past the blunted nose.*

Bob Laburn came slowly out of his daze. Screams and cries were coming from somewhere behind him and he could hear a voice calling out: *"Raus! Raus!"*

He struggled to breathe, gulping for air, still strapped to his seat. I must have hit my chest on my knees, he thought. He tried to straighten himself, but couldn't. Pain shot up his spine to his neck. Something had happened to his back.

Where are my glasses, he wondered, feeling around with his hands. I was wearing them a moment ago, they must be here.

As he was feeling around blindly for his glasses, the man next to him jumped up and dashed away toward the back of the jumbo. Bob Laburn peered at him disappearing down the plane and realized he had to get out of there.

Undoing his seat belt he staggered to his feet. He still couldn't breathe properly and leaned on the seat, looking around. All over the cabin the red roses were still attached to the seats. A woman in the seat directly behind him was not moving, but there was little he could do. He could only walk in a stooped, huddled-up way, and moved off slowly and painfully through the wreckage down the aisle away from the nose.

The floor was tilted downward and stopped in a wide jagged gash where the staircase led to the upper-deck cocktail lounge. A fire had broken out in the hole and Bob Laburn saw flames leaping up about knee-high. But the gap did lead directly out of the wreckage. He shuffled to the edge of the hole and jumped, dropping about ten feet into the flames to land on something soft. Debris was burning fiercely all around him — linings, upholstery

---

* They went to help carry injured passengers away from the starboard side.

and fittings. He pushed through a crack in the bottom of the fuselage and moved away from the plane over the muddy field in front of the starboard wing.

The urge to get away from the plane before it exploded kept him going, but moving was difficult and painful and after about fifty yards he slumped down next to a large stone.

Helmut Frankenberg, forty-four-year-old partner in the Penaten Creme business at Rhoendorf on the Rhine, and his wife Christel, were trapped in their seats. The floor had ripped open beneath them, and the ceiling and parts of the cocktail lounge had fallen down. They were engulfed in wreckage, squeezed between the seats in the dark, barely able to see what was happening.

Footsteps sounded somewhere above their heads, but nobody came. Was it the crew? Christel Frankenberg called again and again.

Her husband, sprawled out next to her and unable to move, felt something wet and shouted: "There's kerosene running over us!"

Christel tried frantically to free herself. She twisted her body, struggled to free her feet and legs. Her husband spoke quietly to her, saying, "Don't panic. Just keep calm. We can only pray that it's all over quickly."

But Christel kept struggling and finally broke free. She pushed herself back out of a hole in the side of the fuselage and fell to the burning ground outside. She looked in through the hole at her husband but he said nothing. He seemed to be unconscious, and she didn't know how to help him.

A man ran through the flames and grabbed her, shouting, "It's going to explode!" He dragged her away as explosions shook the wreck and they ran out together through the smoke and flying metal.

Schacke, the copilot, alarmed by Rudi Hahn's fall down the stairway and the fragile-looking wreckage, headed quickly back to the cockpit. He jumped onto a seat, stretched his hands above his head, and shoved hard up against the sealed overhead hatch.

For a moment nothing happened, and then the hatch opened.

Relieved, Schacke looked out down the port side of the jumbo. He saw flames darting up on the ground below and fire on the left wing. From up there the flames appeared to encircle *Hessen*'s nose and he thought, no, not this exit. Try the other side.

He crossed the cockpit to the jammed service door on the right and struggled with it, sweating as he tried to prise it open. But he couldn't get it to move: something was holding it back.

The copilot decided that he'd have to go through the overhead hatch after all. Grabbing one of the emergency handles, he heaved himself up and through. For a moment he clung to the roof of the cockpit and the whole scene was spread vividly below him. There were small fires all around and the ground was covered with jet fuel. He could see several holes forward of the wing where the fuselage had burst open. Schacke dropped, using his legs and the steel cord of the emergency escape reel to lower himself down the steep side of the jumbo to the ground. Then, from one of the holes in the fuselage, he heard a voice shouting for help. He ran to see what he could do.

As he reached the hole a woman stepped out, hysterical, her clothes torn. Schacke put a hand on her shoulder and urged her quickly away in the direction of other survivors he could see way out past the nose. He turned back, and through one of the holes saw Captain Krack helping a couple trapped in their seats a few yards from the burning wing. The captain, after crawling out of a hole on the far side of the jumbo, had reentered through stewardess Evelyn Rehm's door, somehow managing to climb up the chute between the fleeing passengers. Now, before Schacke could reach Captain Krack, an injured woman covered with blood staggered from the wreckage and collapsed. The copilot ran to help, and tried to drag her away.

He was standing deep in fuel and felt sick and weak from the fumes, afraid he wouldn't make it. He tripped over something and fell, hitting the side of his head. Blood was dripping down from his ear onto his uniform, but he got to his feet, picked the woman up and managed to drag her clear.

Cries were coming from the forward section and Schacke

headed back to the wreckage, but as he approached, two explosions ripped through the jet and flames swirled up over the cabin. The copilot couldn't get any closer — all he could do was watch.

Three rows ahead of the Frankenbergs, Malcolm Solts raised his head. He was covered in debris and dust and still strapped to his seat which was leaning crazily over at an angle, the left side lower than the right. He looked around him in the gloom, trying to see what was left of the 747. He couldn't see very much. All kinds of wreckage blocked his view.

When he looked to his left he realized with a shock that he was almost outside the cabin. The empty seat joined to his had been flung through the side of the jet. There was a gaping crack right next to him and he could see the ground outside and small fires springing up. The twinned seats hung there half-in, half-out, part of a heap of wreckage that rested against the muddy field.

Malcolm Solts shoved aside the wreckage that almost covered him, undid his seat belt and jumped up. He squeezed himself through the hole, dropped down onto the ground, saw fire creeping forward from one of the smashed engines and started to run. He had gone about five or six paces when he heard a man's voice cry, "Help! Help me out!" Hesitating, he looked back and the voice called again.

He knew who it was — the man who had sat behind him, the man from Dusseldorf he'd spent the night talking to up in the cocktail lounge. He turned and ran back.

There were sounds of explosions as Solts crawled in through the cracked fuselage and a sheet of flame shot up. His friend of the night before was covered in wreckage, a huge metal section trapping his legs. Malcolm tried to lift it, pulling frantically, but it wouldn't move. He put his hands under the German's arms and tried to drag him out from under the metal, but it was impossible. The man's legs were tightly wedged.

"Leave me," the man shouted at him. "Get out!"

The fire was right next to them, tongues of flame licking nearer. Malcolm Solts didn't know what to do. The man was trapped; he couldn't get him out. But how could he leave him?

"Get out." The German was pushing him away.

Malcolm stumbled back and saw fire everywhere. He jumped out of the hole he had escaped from minutes before, ducked his head and ran for his life. There were flames spreading across the field outside, climbing high up over the cabin, and thick dark smoke was funneling out of cracks and holes and broken windows. There were more explosions as he ran and he heard the flames crackling behind him. Voices were shouting to him to get away.

Sick with fear and horror he ran out of the smoke. Ahead he saw a group of people standing in the field, their eyes wide, mouths hanging, some sobbing. He went and stood with them.

On the slope nobody said anything. They simply stood and stared, crying as fire engulfed their jet with the people still on board. Christel Frankenberg was standing near the others when the big explosion finally came. Flames spurted up, wrapping the cabin in fire. Christel knew she would never see her husband again.

The Crash Site

SHORTLY BEFORE EIGHT that morning, Gino Iannibelli and two colleagues were standing outside the Italian Sogene Construction Company offices, about half a mile from the runway. They lounged in the fresh morning air, warming themselves in the sun, and looked out over the open expanse of Nairobi airport.

A jet was racing down the runway, a jumbo with a black nose and blue and yellow tail, the name *Lufthansa* standing out clearly on the white-painted body forward of the wing. They heard the roar of the jet as it built up speed for takeoff and waited for the moment when it would thrust itself up from the ground and climb away into the sky.

Gino noticed that the plane seemed to be staying a long time on the ground. It was nearly at the end of the runway. The aircraft lifted but hardly climbed at all — it was so close to the ground. Then it began to fall.

The three men shouted in horror, seeing the plane drop steadily down. They started running to their Land-Rovers without taking their eyes off the terrible sight. Still the jet sank, the tail way down and nearly dragging on the ground. The plane was heading for the road that crossed the line of the runway about half a mile out in the bush.

There was a sudden heavy thud and a spurt of flame as the left wing and engines smashed into the embanked earthwork. Gino watched, horrified, as the jumbo broke apart behind the wings, and then raced to his car with the two others to speed off along the muddy road.

John Kingsley-Heath, the owner of safari companies in Kenya and Botswana, should have been on the Lufthansa flight, but late the previous afternoon he had changed his mind. Catching the Lufthansa jumbo meant getting up at 5.30 or 6 A.M. at the latest — a fairly early start — so he had asked his secretary to see if she could switch his ticket to the British Airways flight that left Nairobi at about 9 A.M. It hadn't been easy, but she'd managed it.

"It was a bit of a rush," she told him when he called in at his office, "but I suppose if it gives you an extra hour's sleep it's all in a good cause." They laughed about it and he took the ticket. He'd had no premonitions, no uneasy feelings, but he'd probably just saved his life.

Check-in time for the British Airways flight was 8 A.M. and shortly before eight, Kingsley-Heath was driving swiftly along the airport road parallel to the runway in his Toyota station wagon. He glanced to his right and saw a 747 — the Lufthansa plane — lifting up off the runway. As the Toyota sped down the road, he watched the plane, his hands gripping the steering wheel, the vehicle aiming itself. He was a commercial pilot with 6,000 hours of flying experience and he could sense something was going wrong.

My God, he thought, the bloody thing's going to stall! I can't believe it's going to get off the ground!

The Toyota almost collided with an oncoming vehicle. He had wandered over into the center of the road and swerved wildly back, braked and swung to the side of the road. When he looked again at the 747 he realized that the plane would crash.

Kingsley-Heath could hear the jet struggling, making a vibrating *chuh-chuh-chuh* noise as it dropped gradually lower with the nose still aimed up. He was staring at it side-on but couldn't see if the undercarriage was extended or retracted. He jumped out of his vehicle and leaped onto the hood. He was standing up there when the 747 went in.

The engines seemed to die away as if they had been switched off. There was a tremendous sound as it impacted, a cloud of glass or loose sand flew up, and the 747 shot forward.

Kingsley-Heath jumped down off the Toyota, got back inside, slammed it into gear and roared off up a dirt road in the direction of the crash. The station wagon bounced and jerked over the rough ground. He could see burning wreckage ahead.

The Toyota was the first vehicle on the scene. Kingsley-Heath drew up about two hundred yards from the plane, worried that the wreckage might explode and hurl fire everywhere. He jumped out and started running. The size of the aircraft and the extent of the wreckage appalled him and he faltered, suddenly wondering just what he should do. And then he saw the first survivors.

They were wandering around the burning wreckage, dazed and bewildered, their clothing torn and muddied. Nearby lay about twenty contorted bodies, many of them charred and burned. As Kingsley-Heath went forward to see how he could help, people were streaming toward the area from all directions, some running from the direction of Nairobi airport, others coming up from the road. He looked back down the long groove scraped in the ground by the jumbo's belly and saw debris and suitcases and wrecked luggage. People in the crowd were stooping and looting. He thought irrationally, if I had my gun with me I'd probably shoot them.

Gino Iannibelli and his two friends were there in minutes. They turned their Land-Rovers off the road and drove bouncing over the bush, stopped, jumped down and ran to the wreck.

It was a terrible scene. There were bodies, pieces of metal and shredded luggage lying everywhere they looked. In the middle of it all lay what was left of the jumbo: the "head" of the aircraft, black smoke streaming out of it, and fire spreading along the left wing.

The three Italians ran in, put their arms around a group of stumbling and wounded survivors and dragged them away from the flames as another explosion shook the wreck.

They returned to the plane again and again, picking up some who could not walk and running with them to safety. Those who were unconscious they laid at the side of the embanked road to await the ambulances they could hear screaming in the distance. How many of these, Gino thought in despair, are already dead?

A short distance away from the wreck he found a blonde-haired little girl, not much older than three, wearing a red suit. She was lying motionless, her small head turned sideways on the ground. As he looked at her everything broke inside him. He started crying.

"Come here," he shouted to his friends.

One of them came over, knelt down and felt for the little girl's pulse. For a moment the man held the tiny wrist in his hand and then placed it gently back at her side. He looked at Gino.

"She is dead," he said quietly.

Gino turned away and wiped his eyes. He felt his courage going. It was too much for a soul to bear. He began walking heavily, eyes burning, back to his car.

Among the hundreds of people running to the scene was press photographer Samuel Ouma of the Nairobi *Daily Nation*, who had been at the airport to photograph the West German Bundestag members who had flown in from Frankfurt aboard the Lufthansa jumbo.

After the pictures were taken and the Bundestag team set off on their short drive to the city, Samuel Ouma went over to the airport bar for an early morning beer, his camera slung from his shoulder. He had been there only a few minutes when he heard screams and shouts: "The jumbo has crashed!"

People began to run from the building and Samuel Ouma ran after them, his unfinished beer standing on the bar. He headed for the runway and saw a dense black column of smoke rising into the sky near the Mombasa road.

He took pictures as he ran, the telephoto lens zooming right to the horrible scene: the jet lying belly-down and keeled over in the mud, the black nose aiming back the way it had been traveling, and flames flaring up from the wing, high over the cabin. Dark clouds piled up on each other, billowing and swirling way above it all.

By now, hundreds of people were heading for the embanked earth road. Ahead Samuel could see a trail of wreckage and bodies, and as he focused his camera he heard voices crying out for help. But there were others already helping, dashing into the torn metal and dragging people out, and he kept squeezing the shutter release, clicking off picture after picture. The pictures composed themselves: twisted wreckage, shocked faces of survivors, curling smoke, the grotesque poses of the dead. Later these appalling sights would be flashed around the world. By nightfall the horror he had just seen through his lens would be shared with millions as newspapers splashed his photographs across their front pages and television networks beamed them into the homes of people in countries he had never seen.

But Samuel Ouma didn't think about that now. Shocked by the scenes around him, he felt ill. It was the sort of thing you read about in books or saw in films. He had never expected to see it in real life on a peaceful morning like this.

About thirty yards out in the field a small group of survivors collected, examining each other for injuries. John Bing looked in amazement at Terry Partridge and his briefcase.

"It fell into my lap when we crashed," Terry explained.

As he watched the jumbo burning, Terry noticed the back half of the plane was missing and realized that the crash had been worse then he had thought. Some people must have been killed. And it shocked him to think he could have been one of them.

A man's voice called out for help. He was lying on the ground next to the jumbo, clutching his back. The Bings and Terry Partridge and some of the others ran back down the slight slope to see what they could do.

"My back," the man said. "I can't move my back."

Terry looked at him and thought, he might have broken it. We shouldn't try to move him.

"He should stay lying down until the ambulance comes," Jean Bing, a radiographer, said. "He shouldn't be moved." But after discussion, they agreed to move the man at least away from the wreck — there might be more explosions and fire.

Terry Partridge rolled up his jacket, kneeled down, and gently placed it under the man's head while the others, including a Lufthansa steward, searched for a board or something to carry him on. A fiberglass sheet was found in the wreckage and brought over, and they got the wounded man onto it and carried him carefully away.

A Land-Rover drew up and a man jumped down and shouted: "Put him in the back. I'll take him to the hospital."

They loaded the man into the car and someone climbed in next to him. The small group watched the Land-Rover move slowly off over the bush. No one spoke. The three of them walked on, feeling confused and lost, toward the earth road strewn with wreckage. There were crowds of people up there, silhouetted against the early morning sky.

Gino Iannibelli met the group as he was heading sadly back to his car. He saw a middle-aged couple and a young man stumbling unsteadily through the wreckage. The woman had lost a shoe and was having difficulty walking over the tufted grass and the man, probably her husband, had lost his jacket. The younger man had all his clothes and carried a briefcase. All of them, Gino noticed, seemed dazed and deeply shocked and moved strangely.

He couldn't speak English, so he pointed up the slope and mimed the question, "Do you want something warm to drink?" He led them to his Land-Rover, helped them in, and drove off up the embanked road to the Sogene Construction Company's staff canteen. One of the firm's English consultants came to help, sat them down and made them a cup of tea.

"I was in the D-Day landing in Normandy," he said, shaking his head, "but seeing that plane come down was worse than anything that happened there."

Back at the crash site, Hermann Hennecke was stumbling

around the bush. He heard voices and made out six people approaching.

"Could you please help me to the airport," he called out. "I've lost my glasses and I can't see very well."

The six survivors came over to join him, but stood without speaking, watching the flames shooting up from the jumbo. In the distance they could hear sirens wailing and shrieking but none of them reacted. It was as if they were outsiders and had never been on *Hessen* at all.

After a while the group turned and began walking toward the embanked earth road in the distance. At the road one of the survivors stopped a car and asked the driver to take them back to the airport.

"Get in," he urged and opened the doors.

Hermann Hennecke and the other six got in and sat tightly hunched together as the car began to edge away through the crowds. Hennecke turned to take one last look at *Hessen*. For the first time he felt an overwhelming sense of gratitude.

Bob Laburn, his shoes thick with clay, lay on the ground, resting on his left elbow, trying to find a position that would ease the pain in his back and neck. Nothing seemed to help. Any slight movement brought agony.

Others who had escaped were standing in the scattered remains of luggage and paper and pieces of wreckage that lay around him. Some appeared to be unhurt but others were staggering and limping, looking back at the fiercely burning 747. Heat was blistering and blackening the paintwork.

A figure approached and sat down on Bob Laburn's stone. Laburn looked up, saw a man with blood running from a gash in his right cheek, recognized him, and called out: "Hello John, fancy meeting you here."

It was John Hall, general manager of Southern Cross Steel in Johannesburg who had met him many times before on business. The two men were unaware they had been on the same flight until they found each other here in a strange African field thousands of miles from home in torn and bloodstained clothing and with a blazing jet for a backdrop. It was a bizarre setting.

"Are you badly hurt?"

"No, I'm all right," John Hall touched his cheek, "except for this. But it's not serious."

John had escaped down an emergency chute on the starboard side. Sitting directly behind him in the economy class cabin had been his managing director and business colleague Anthony Grant, and he had not seen him since the plane had gone down.

A Land-Rover was moving slowly through the wreckage and Bob Laburn saw some men picking up survivors and helping the injured. When one of the men came over and tried to lift him into the Land-Rover another survivor intervened.

"Leave him until an ambulance comes," Herbert Frosch told them. "He's injured his back, we should be careful how we move him."

Bob Laburn remained half-lying in the center of the small group of people, gritting his teeth against the pain.

People were still running away from the wreck but they were now being passed by hundreds of Kenyans going the other way. Fearful of a huge explosion, all those who had been on the jet were trying to get as far away as they could, while the Africans kept moving closer and closer, many running right in among the wreckage and injured. Some went to help, carrying and dragging survivors out on their backs, others went to loot, snatching often worthless items from the debris.

West German diplomatic courier Knut Müller had been heading south to Pretoria with a sealed diplomatic bag. He had jumped from the jumbo and started running when a blast caught him and seemed to lift him off his feet. He blacked out.

When he came to he was lying in the mud close to the wrecked jumbo, unable to move because of the pain of his injuries. A black man was standing over him. The man took his tie and tried to pull the shoes from his feet.

Knut Müller cried out for help.

A fellow survivor ran back and the looter made off clutching the tie. Knut never saw it again, or the diplomatic bag he had been carrying. For the next few days German officials would search the accident site, probing the ground with steel rods and sifting through the burned-out wreckage for the secret coding machine the bag had contained. They found no sign of it.

Captain Heinz Peper from Busdorf in Schleswig, had been on his way to Durban to take command of the container ship *Pallas*. Knocked flat by an explosion as he was fleeing the burning jet, he regained consciousness to find himself lying on the ground. Looters were searching through the pockets of the dead and injured near him, taking passports, wallets, travelers' checks, watches, rings and money. Too shocked to speak or cry out, he watched the looters coming toward him and felt hands feeling in his pockets. They took everything he had — even his captain's card.

We stood, weepy and shaken, four people on a slight rise in that muddy field, looking back at the wreck. Sirens were screaming some way off in the distance. The flames were right over the cabin we had escaped from. I thought of the blood-smeared old man we had left in the seat behind us and felt sick with anguish. He was still in that mess.

"All those poor people," my wife was crying. "Those poor people."

We had not seen more than eight other survivors. Where were all the rest? A dozen people all told — were we the only ones who got out? It was so difficult to believe what was happening. At that moment we should have been sitting comfortably in our seats thousands of feet in the sky, jetting on toward Johannesburg. But here we were in a muddy field we had never seen before, and all we had were our lives. Everything else was going up in smoke — our clothes, passports, money, papers and cameras.

"I knew it, I knew it," Lynn cried.

We held each other and the children and I thought, my God, we were so close to dying, so close. But we made it — a few rows

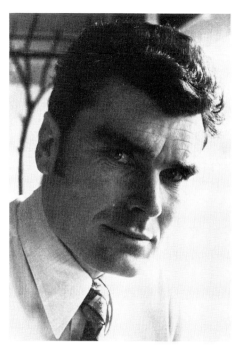

(*above left*) Flight Engineer Rudi Hahn. (*right*) Copilot Joachim Schacke.
(*below left*) Check Purser Jurgen Freund. (*right*) Steward Tom Scott
(*Stern*)

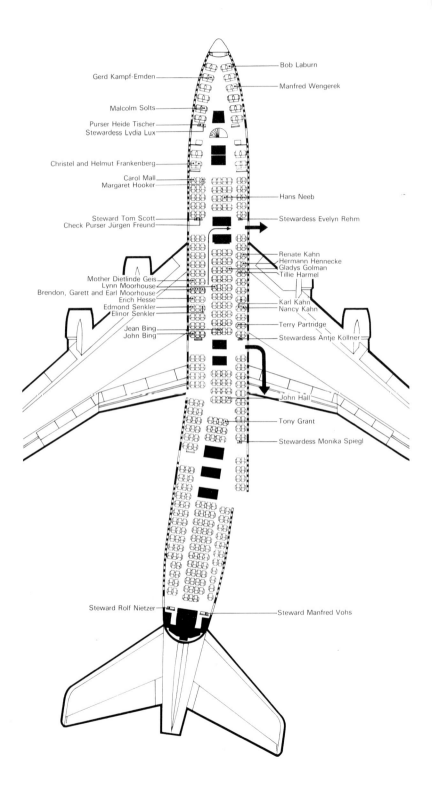

Gerd Kampf-Emden

Bob Laburn

Manfred Wengerek

Malcolm Solts

Purser Heide Tischer
Stewardess Lydia Lux

Christel and Helmut Frankenberg

Carol Mall
Margaret Hooker

Hans Neeb

Steward Tom Scott
Check Purser Jurgen Freund

Stewardess Evelyn Rehm

Renate Kahn
Hermann Hennecke
Gladys Golman
Tillie Harmel

Mother Dietlinde Geis
Lynn Moorhouse
Brendon, Garett and Earl Moorhouse
Erich Hesse
Edmond Senkler
Elinor Senkler

Karl Kahn
Nancy Kahn

Jean Bing
John Bing

Terry Partridge

Stewardess Antje Kollner

John Hall

Tony Grant

Stewardess Monika Spiegl

Steward Rolf Nietzer

Steward Manfred Vohs

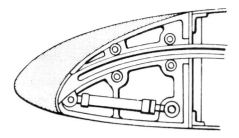

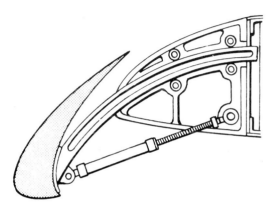

(*above*) The leading edge flap in retracted and extended position. *Hessen* took off with both flaps retracted, which caused the jet to stall only 100 feet from the ground

(*left*) Seating plan of *Hessen* showing the location of passengers mentioned in the text

(*above*) Stewardess Lydia Lux. (*below*) Purser Heide Tischer (*Stern*)

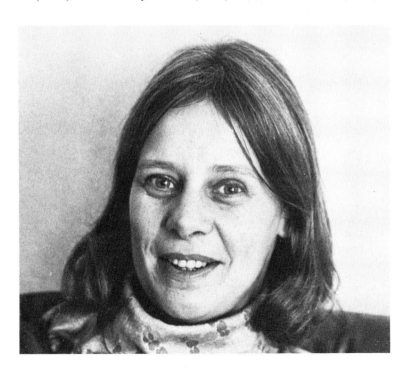

further back and we wouldn't be standing here now. Why were *we* saved?

Then a group of what were obviously survivors staggered up, a man and two women and, not far behind them, another two women. It was a relief to see them. We could hear they were Americans from their accents. The three in front, we found out later, were Karl, Renate and Nancy Kahn, and the two women helping each other along, sisters Tillie Harmel and Gladys Golman, all struggling together through the muddy African bush. The earth was caked onto them, their eyes were wide and their faces taut. Tillie Harmel carried a shoe in her hand and was breathing harshly, her mouth wide open, and clutching her side.

"Are you all right?" I called out, but no one answered the question.

They stopped and looked back.

"Where are all the people?" Renate Kahn asked. "Surely we can't be the only ones who got out."

We stared down the slope but all we could see were crowds of Africans and beyond them the wreck.

"There must be others somewhere."

With a rumbling noise a gray Land-Rover came bucking and bouncing over the bush. It drew up next to us and a man leaned from the window and shouted: "Are any of you hurt?"

"We're all right," one of the Americans called out. "Just a little shaken up."

"Have you got a cigarette?" Nancy Kahn asked him. "Please, I must have a cigarette." She felt terribly shaky and needed one badly.

A cigarette was passed through the car window and one of the men inside lit it for her. Nancy inhaled deeply, eyes closed, as if her whole being was centered on that cigarette. She had never known such craving.

"Climb in," the man said. "I'll take you all back to the airport."

"Don't worry about us. We're all right. Why don't you see if you can help those people down at the plane?"

The Land-Rover moved off down the hill and at that moment

the airport fire engines finally came nosing through between the people, sirens blaring, and closed in on the burning wreck.

The heat kept the firemen back but they got two engines in next to the burning wing, another two up ahead of the nose and sprayed foam into the flames. Nearby stood a rescue vehicle with cutting equipment, but there was little those men could do.

From the hill we could see the foam jetting out in arcs, and the crowds of Africans surrounding the plane. The fire had been sucked into the cockpit, drawn through by the open crew escape hatch in the road, and dense black smoke streamed out. The jet was now a tube of fire — the firemen were too late.

A few minutes behind the fire brigade came the ambulances, and the fight to save the injured began.

Malcolm Solts came limping up to join the survivors gathered together ahead of *Hessen*'s blunted nose, not far from the embanked road. His legs were cut and badly bruised and there was something wrong with his right knee. Each time he bent it pain stabbed his leg.

People looked bewildered and stared blankly; no one was saying anything. The only noise was the crackling of flames and explosions coming from the 747.

Groups of people were darting through the wreckage picking up items of value, sometimes passing right by struggling survivors.

A ragged line of uniformed men armed with automatic rifles and clubs suddenly appeared, members of the military General Service Unit which had a camp in the area. Now as Malcolm Solts watched, the brown-shirted soldiers fired into the air and charged. There was a terrible scramble to get away. Looters went sprawling in the mud and others ran right over them. They jumped up and ran wildly on up the slope in a crowd, making shrill cries of alarm as the soldiers moved in behind them. About thirty yards out from the wreck the Unit halted and cordoned the area off. No more looters could get near.

One person who did not see the looters or the arrival of the soldiers was Carol Mall. The American woman from the Agency for International Development in Addis Ababa lay gravely injured on her back in the center of a huddle of people. The last thing she would remember when she woke up was the jumbo beginning to crumple and then the voice of her fellow passenger Margaret Hooker saying to her, "We'll get you out, Carol. We'll get you out." After that, nothing.

Margaret Hooker sat near Carol Mall nursing her gashed foot, watching as the men who had helped to carry Carol from the wreck tried to make her comfortable on the ground. One of them tried to raise her head so they could slide a handbag under her but she cried out in pain. Her reaction startled them and they decided to leave her lying as she was. No one realized then that she had broken her neck.

Margaret was distracted by a Lufthansa stewardess pointing at her arm. She looked down and saw a deep cut near the elbow, the flesh hanging open, but very little blood. Surprisingly she hadn't felt anything. The stewardess passed her an airline scarf and she bound the wound together, knotting the ends of the material.

Next to her sat the uniformed man she had seen running past while she was still trapped in the jumbo. He was trying to cheer everyone up.

"I bet you could do with a cup of tea," he said to her.

"Never mind the cup of tea," Margaret told him. "I could do with a drink!"

The man laughed and a few of the others smiled.

An ambulance drove up and a group of people who had been helping at the wreck ran up carrying a young child about two years old dressed in a jumper suit. The child was unconscious and they placed her gently in the back of the ambulance.

A doctor who had come with the ambulance and several first-aid workers examined Carol Mall. The doctor tugged at her sweater, trying to pull it away from the upper arm so he could give her a shot but the action tightened the sweater against her neck. She groaned in pain and the doctor quickly let go and rolled up her sleeve instead.

The helpers had brought down a stretcher and together they moved Carol carefully onto it, lifted her up and put her in the ambulance. Margaret Hooker climbed into the back, sat down and braced herself as the vehicle began to move, siren wailing, over the rough ground toward the asphalt road crowded with sightseers' cars.

Wandering bewildered across the bush, Edmund and Elinor Senkler headed for the embanked road in the distance. Elinor picked up a piece of metal about the size of a candy bar and ran her hands over its smooth surface.

"We're alive! A miracle!" she said again and again as they walked. They had come out of a crash like that with hardly a scratch.

She carried the metal a few paces and dropped it back on the ground. They passed an engine cowling and saw the shallow dent where it had struck the earth.

As they walked they met Captain Krack and another crew member both talking with a survivor who was an amateur pilot. Edmund Senkler listened to the conversation and added his own impressions.

"It felt like someone had pulled down the rear flaps," Edmund told the pilot.

"Impossible!" Captain Krack shook his head. "Everything was normal. I can't understand what happened."

"There didn't appear to be any power failure," Edmund said.

Captain Krack agreed. He lapsed into a troubled silence and that was the end of the discussion. They walked on, each alone in his thoughts.

The Lucky Ones

TOM SCOTT STOOD watching the fire, his emotions in turmoil. He was elated that he had saved so many and had survived himself, but noticing the tail section lying in jagged pieces all over the bush, he knew deep down that all his friends in there had been killed.

He was standing there thinking bitter, somber thoughts when an American woman came over to him.

"Now my trip is ruined!" she complained. "This crash has ruined everything."

Tom looked at her, speechless.

"Lady," he said angrily, "you should be glad you're alive."

The woman turned and walked away and Tom Scott thought, maybe it's shock. It must be shock. No one would behave like that normally.

Scott left the survivors and went to help the ambulance men who were carrying the wounded away. There weren't very many seriously hurt, but there were lots of people with gashed heads and bleeding cuts; people were limping, holding their chests and backs, their faces contorted with pain. He helped as many as he could, walking with them through the debris to the ambulances.

When they had all gone he stood on the embanked road staring at the firemen pouring foam onto the wreck.

A man in a car asked if he wanted a lift to the airport. Tom looked at him and got into the car. There was nothing more he could do. He buckled the seat belt tightly across his hips and the car rolled slowly down off the earth road to the Mombasa highway.

"Please drive very carefully," Tom Scott pleaded. "I've just been through a really shaking, nerve-wracking experience."

"Don't worry," the man told him.

But Tom, feeling terribly nervous, repeated his request three or four times during the short ride to Nairobi airport.

The Land-Rover came back up the hill to fetch us. There was nothing they could do down at the wreck, the driver told us. The firemen and ambulance crews had taken over.

We helped the children into the back and climbed in next to them. It was crowded; there were ten of us in there including the driver. He put the vehicle in gear and we rumbled, jerked, and bounced over the bush and turned onto the embanked earth road. It was smoother after that, but we still drove slowly. The Land-Rover drew up and stopped almost in line with *Hessen*'s nose and we saw it all spread out to our left. There were torn pieces of metal on the top of the road and a shallow groove where the jet had gone over. Immediately below us was a dark oily smudge, the site of the first explosion, and what was left of the tail section where so many people had been sitting. They had died here below us. We, the lucky ones, had gone hurtling on, spun around and come nosing back to stop where the remains of *Hessen* now stood.

Wreckage, shredded clothing, metal and suitcases were lying everywhere. Sitting on a mound was the little nun and a stewardess in her bright yellow uniform. Survivors were milling about, some climbing the side of the road.

"I can see dead bodies over there," my son Brendon called out.

"No, you can't," my wife told him.

"I can," he insisted, "Over there."

When Heidi Tischer saw our children in the Land-Rover she ran over in tears. "Have you seen the Mickey Mouse?" she asked. "We can't find the Mickey Mouse."

"No," Lynn told her. "The children were sitting with us."

"They weren't with the Mickey Mouse?"

"No, I'm sorry. They were with us all the time."

Heidi Tischer turned away, crying.

From below an American voice shouted: "Unitours? Anyone from the Unitours party?"

Renate Kahn shouted back the names of the five Americans in the Land-Rover: "We're five up here — Karl, Nancy and Renate Kahn and Gladys Golman and Tillie Harmel. Who have you got?"

A voice down there called out five names and there was some talk we could not make out.

"What did they say?" someone in the Land-Rover asked.

"Three are missing," Renate told us. "The Solibakkes and Maya, our guide."

We fell silent. There was nothing you could say, nothing at all.

Our driver friend climbed back in. "Everybody all right?"

"Yes," I said quietly, answering for us all.

The Land-Rover's engine rumbled back to life, the wheels crunched over the wreckage on the road, and down we headed toward the airport.

The first of the ambulances raced back along the road to Nairobi, swerving out wildly on the two-lane highway to overtake slower moving traffic. Most of the cars were traveling the other way, the people attracted by the dark column of smoke that could be seen from the city. The long line of cars coming head-on created a new hazard for the already shaken survivors.

Dr. Gerd Kampf-Emden held on as the ambulance slowed and swerved and braked. There was one other injured person in there with him, but the two of them did not talk much, waiting nervously for the journey to be over. Dr. Kampf-Emden stared down at his bleeding right foot, surprised that he had not felt anything back there at the crash site. His friend Hans Neeb had pointed out that one of the Lufthansa slippers that he had put on so he could relax during the flight was covered in blood. His shoes, back there on the jet, he thought wryly, were probably ashes by now.

Further back along the road came the ambulance carrying Margaret Hooker and Carol Mall. They had traveled this road together heading for the airport just over an hour ago, talking about Carol's holiday in South Africa. Now Margaret sat in silence and stared at the limp body of the little girl in the jumper and wondered, "Is that child alive?" It lay so still, unmoving and deathly white that she couldn't believe it was.

Carol Mall, lying on the other side of the ambulance, stirred. For a moment the darkness lifted and she saw the roof of the ambulance and heard the siren screaming up ahead. She blinked her eyes, and sank slowly back into unconsciousness. It would be seven days before she came to and life would never be the same again.

Back at the wreck Herbert Frosch and a group of helpers pulled a piece of board from the debris and carefully maneuvered Bob Laburn onto it. An ambulance stopped close by and the small group of men lifted him up, carried him over and placed him in the back.

"You should lie flat out," someone suggested.

But Bob Laburn found that too painful. His half-reclining position looked peculiar but it eased the throbbing a little.

The doors slammed shut and he was alone in the ambulance. He heard the ambulancemen getting in up front, there was a rumbling as the engine started and the hell ride began. Each bump and jolt and rise and fall sent a jarring shock up his spine to the base of his skull. He closed his eyes and clenched his teeth, but the ride went on and on, the agony exploding with each lurch of the springs. He prayed for it to be over soon.

Once he heard the men talking.

"This man has an injured back," he heard a voice saying. "We must take him to the nearest hospital, not Nairobi."

The voices droned on ahead but he concentrated on the

swaying, leaning on his arm to lessen the impact. It didn't seem to help. How much longer, he asked himself. If only we were on a decent road, maybe it would not be so bad.

He couldn't see where they were going and he had no idea of time or distance. At times it felt as if they had been traveling for hours over the bumpy road, but judging by the conversation of the ambulancemen they couldn't have been. We've probably not gone very far at all, he told himself, but this is the worst journey of my life.

The ride became smoother and the ambulance stopped. He heard the men walking around, the doors opened and sunlight streamed in. They had arrived at the Mater Misericordiae Catholic mission hospital a few miles from the crash site.

The men picked him up and carried him in and the Irish and Kenyan sisters came hurrying up to examine him. Within a few minutes Bob Laburn was settled on a bed, pleased that the ride was over, but anxious about his family down in Johannesburg. He should let them know he was alive.

He told Sister Leonard who was making him comfortable: "Don't worry about me, but can you please telephone my wife or the Rand Water Board in Johannesburg and tell them I'm reasonably all right?"

The sister went off to see what she could do. Later she came back. She hadn't been able to get through, the telephone lines to South Africa were jammed with calls.

That wasn't very surprising, Bob Laburn thought. Communications between the two countries weren't very good on normal days, never mind on days like this.

"Would it be possible for you to send a telegram to my office and tell them Bob Laburn is well?" he asked.

"Yes," the sister said. "I can do that."

He gave her the address and a rough wording and off she went.

After an hour she returned. The telegram had gone off; his family and friends should hear the good news within an hour or so.

"Right," Bob Laburn said, "now you can deal with me."

The hospital's orthopedic surgeon and an Asian radiologist examined him carefully. He had three crushed dorsal vertebrae, some cervical spine difficulty, a crushed chest and some pneumonia in one lung. But he felt reasonably content now that news was on its way to his family. They would soon hear and stop worrying.

He had no way of knowing that his telegram would only arrive a whole day later, and that neither hospital nor ambulance staff had reported his arrival at the mission hospital. For a long time his family and Lufthansa officials feared he was dead.

A bus drew up at the scene of the wreck and the survivors straggled over to it and began to climb aboard. Edmund and Elinor Senkler sat down beside the little nun.

"Where are the sisters?" Mother Dietlinde asked. She looked troubled and had a red lump on her forehead.

Elinor took her hand and comforted her. The other sisters had been sitting in the rear compartment and that, Elinor knew, had been destroyed.

Across the aisle sat Captain Krack, holding his head in his hands, going over and over the details of the takeoff with one of the passengers.

The seats filled up and the bus started. It moved off slowly and as it drew level with the smoking wreck Captain Krack got up, stopped it and jumped off.

"I can't understand it," he muttered to himself again and again.

The survivors watched him walking, head down on his chest, toward the wreckage as the bus moved slowly on.

Shock

THE CAR CARRYING Dancy Bruce and Esther Burton drew up in front of Embakasi Airport. They got out with Jock Leslie-Melville and the three of them stood there, pale and shaken by what they had seen a few minutes ago, riding in along the airport road.

They looked for a porter to help them with the luggage but there were none in sight on this early Wednesday morning. The porters along with other airport officials were, at the moment they arrived, running wildly across the bush to the scene of the wreck.

Jock and the two young women picked up the luggage and struggled awkwardly into the terminal building. They dumped their bags in a heap in front of the check-in desk. There was no one behind the desk, no one behind any of the desks.

Dancy looked around. Over at the coffee bar the assistants had disappeared and the people in the lounge had climbed behind the bar to make their own coffee. There was no uniformed staff anywhere, only people walking up and down, pacing the smooth stone floor, horror in their faces, some crying, holding the hands of friends, covering their eyes.

They were standing there looking at the chaotic scene, their own shocked faces adding to it, when a friend of Dancy's, Bruce

Hobson, walked up clutching a newspaper in his hand. He looked upset. Dancy felt the whole thing was like being in a horror movie that had no director.

"Bruce," she said, holding him, "have you seen, have you heard about the crash?"

"Yes," he said, looking at her. "I was on the observation deck —" He shook his head.

Bruce Hobson worked for a Nairobi safari company and earlier that morning had escorted four German clients to the airport to catch the Lufthansa flight to Johannesburg. They were happy and relaxed, chatting and joking in the bus about their African holiday. No one seemed to be concerned about flying.

He had marshaled them through the check-in, helped them to organize their seats and luggage, and directed them through immigration and customs. There had been handshakes at the barrier, smiles and last-minute greetings. They had gone walking away toward the exit. And that was the last Bruce had seen of them.

In half an hour or so his friend Dancy Bruce would be catching her flight to London and he'd decided to wait around. He bought a newspaper and went up to the first floor to sit on the observation balcony and he'd been sitting there in the early morning sun reading when it happened.

There were screams and shouts. People cried out suddenly, gasped.

Bruce looked up and saw everyone moving to the right, pressing and pushing to see something.

He jumped up and saw beyond the heads of the crowd, a ball of fire and thick dark smoke billowing upward. The plane's crashed, he thought, stunned, and it hit him — my clients. They're in that!

He turned away, shaken, and hurried downstairs — he had to find out what had happened, what had gone wrong.

At the bottom of the stairs he found himself part of an incredible scene. Ticket collectors, customs officers, every single airline official it seemed, was running through the baggage hall in the direction of the runway. Behind them came passengers and spectators streaming through, dropping suitcases, bags and belongings all over the reception area as they ran. Above the shouts and cries came a high-pitched and agitated voice of a woman over the public address system announcing that the jumbo had just crashed.

Betty, Jock thought suddenly, I should telephone Betty. She might hear something on the radio and think it's Dancy's plane.

He went off and found a telephone and dialed his wife's number.

Betty Leslie-Melville did not understand him at first.

"It was awful," he said. "Terrible. I've never seen anything like it. All those people."

"What was it?" she asked, thinking, it's a bus smash. These awful roads.

"A jumbo," he said. "A 747 crashed at the airport."

"Oh my God."

Jock told her what he had seen, reliving it in his mind as he spoke into the telephone, the great jet floating on down, sinking, and the huge red fireball erupting over the bush.

"There just couldn't have been any survivors —"

There was a silence on the phone.

Then Betty spoke. "What is Dancy going to do?"

"She says she'll go on to London. She feels that chances are against there being two crashes on the same day and I agree with her. They've closed the airport for the moment, but the runway isn't affected. They're sure to open it again soon." Jock paused, hearing the airport noises around him, and then he thought of something that hit him like a physical blow. He shook uncontrollably and a cold shiver climbed up his back.

"Betty," he said hoarsely, "that could be the Moorhouses' plane."

Dancy Bruce's bags kept her place in the long line of people building up in front of the charter flight check-in desk. The new arrivals, probably some of them people who had not heard about the tragedy, were angry that their flight was being held up. There was arguing in the line and voices were raised.

"Look," Dancy heard someone saying, "you can't expect your plane to leave while they're still trying to find out what's happened to the one that's crashed."

Sickened by it, Dancy strolled off to one side with Bruce and Esther. Jock had gone, headed back to his office in the center of Nairobi to see what he could find out. Only minutes away from her flight, Dancy kept telling herself, it can't happen twice on the same day at the same airport. It just can't. The odds are totally against it. But she couldn't stop worrying and felt sick to her stomach. She knew this flight would be the worst she'd ever been on. But she had to go, or she might never be able to climb onto an aircraft again.

A voice came over the public address system and people turned their heads to listen. Some of the officials must have come back to the airport, Dancy thought. The voice was inviting people who wanted to telephone South Africa to assemble in one of the airport rooms. It was an unusual announcement in a country that normally would have nothing to do with South Africa, but this was an unusual day.

Doctors and nurses came hurrying into the airport and all eyes followed. And then, about forty minutes after the jumbo had gone crashing down, Dancy saw the first survivors arriving.

A Land-Rover drew up outside the airport entrance. It was splashed with mud and pieces of grass were sticking to the tires. The doors swung open and a group of people got out and walked slowly into the airport. Leading them was a bizarre trio, two men and a woman, one of the men white-haired and deathly pale and trembling so violently that the others had to hold him up. There was blood coming from his ears and dripping down onto his shirt, and next to him walked a woman, tall and elderly, head up and smiling as she came in. There were small cuts on their faces and they all seemed to have bits of fluff hanging in their hair and on their shoulders and down on their clothes.

Out of a second Land-Rover more people came bunched and stumbling into the airport. They were helping along a stewardess who was crying and sobbing hysterically, her bright yellow jacket clutched tightly to her, mud and spots of blood staining the white of her blouse. They walked unsteadily, clothes torn, and ashen faces with wide staring eyes. They had fluff all over them and had difficulty walking. Great clods of grassy mud covered their shoes and stockinged feet, marking out a trail from the Land-Rovers over the smooth airport floor.

A long-haired young woman came wandering by, both her shoes missing, leading two young boys in red pullovers. The three of them drifted by, plodding blindly on through the staring people. They passed close by Dancy and it seemed they didn't know who to go to, or where to go, or what to say or do. They looked totally lost and bewildered, horror etched in their silent faces, and Dancy felt, I should help them or speak to them or something. But she didn't know what to do and stood numbed, watching them walk jerkily away and vanish into the airport building.

No more people came after the first two Land-Rovers arrived and Dancy thought with a sick empty feeling, ten lucky people made it. Only ten.

Dancy was wrong. There were already seven survivors at the airport when the first Land-Rovers drew up. Hermann Hennecke and his six German-speaking companions had arrived by car and were wandering about the building looking for telephones. Their one thought was to let their families know they were all right. They were spotted by Taj Gulam, Lufthansa's passenger service manager for East Africa, and escorted through to a cafeteria off the departure concourse. Looking shaken himself, Taj urged them to sit down and relax at the small tables and order something hot to drink — at the airline's expense.

Hennecke and his companions sat down and a small team of first-aid workers hovered about them, cleaning out and dressing their few scratches and wounds. The group was joined by stewardesses waiting for the incoming British Airways flight. Taj

Gulam moved among the tables with a clipboard and ballpoint pen and, speaking gently, took down the names and addresses.

"If there is any close relative you would like us to telex, please give me the name and address," he said.

Hermann Hennecke wrote down his name and slipped out of the room. He walked down a passage and turned into an office and asked the man behind the desk if he could use the telephone.

"I have just survived the crash," he told the man, "and I would like to contact my family to tell them I'm okay."

"What crash?" the man asked, amazed. He had sat through all the announcements and turmoil and hadn't heard a thing.

When Hermann Hennecke told him, the man's eyes widened and he began to shake his head. He stared down at Hermann's feet. There was a ball of mud on each foot.

Hermann helped himself to the telephone directory, looked up his firm's Nairobi agents, and dialed the number. The Kenyan still stared dumbly at him.

He heard the voice of Hartmeier, the local sales representative: "Who is that?"

"Hennecke, Olympia South Africa," he answered. "My plane has just crashed."

The voice laughed in his ear. "You're a real joker!"

"No, this is deadly serious," Hermann insisted. "Will you please come to the airport. I must telephone my family in Johannesburg and Germany as soon as possible and I don't think it will be possible from here. I've also lost my glasses."

The voice on the other end of the line was no longer laughing.

"I'll be there in about twenty minutes."

Hennecke left the office and walked through the airport, not knowing where he was heading or why. He saw a bar in a corner, went up and ordered himself a neat brandy. A man he had never seen before paid the bill. Hermann's money, along with his jacket and briefcase, were probably going up in smoke at that very moment.

He felt the warmth of the brandy spreading through him and thought, it's only money. It could have been me.

SURVIVORS

John and Jean Bing

Bob Laburn

Mother Dietlinde Geis

Elinor Senkler

Terry Partridge

Carol Mall

Hans Neeb

Edmund Senkler

Erich Hesse

Hermann Hennecke

Margaret Hooker

Dr. Gerd Kampf-Emden

Nancy Khan

Renate and Karl Khan

Earl and Lynn Moorhouse with their two sons, Garett and Brendon, at Nairobi airport immediately after the crash

We wandered through the airport, Lynn with the two boys, myself, and the five Americans. Everything seemed remote and insubstantial, even the sounds had a new quality — flat and muted, as if someone had padded the place with cotton wool.

The people standing in the building stared at us as we came through, but we were too shocked to feel self-conscious. We looked at them without really seeing them, and went on by, trapped in the turmoil of our minds. We were all moving jerkily and deliberately, taking giant strides, yet almost floating, as if we were stepping over rolled-up carpets on the floor.

The nurses helping in the cafeteria where the survivors were gathering knew what it was. Some of them came out to help us in, put their arms around us, supported us, and sat us down at the tables. A British Airways stewardess in a pink uniform ran her hand over the boys' heads.

"Were they hurt?"

"No." We shook our heads.

"Brendon was sleeping," Lynn said in a strange voice.

"And you? Are any of you hurt?"

"My back's killing me," Lynn said, holding herself. "I think I've slipped a disk or something."

The stewardess looked alarmed and one of the nurses came over. While she was glancing over the others I examined myself. There was a cut on one of my fingers from the plastic ceiling and a gash on my leg, probably from hitting the seat when we struck the ground. I had my trouser leg pulled up to look and the stewardess saw it and said: "Oh, we must fix that up."

But it was nothing, the blood was already drying, and I told her, "Don't worry about it. It's all right."

But she insisted, went off and came back with a bandage and I thought well, let her put it on then if it gives her something to do. She looks pretty shaken up. Maybe she wants to keep her mind off flying.

"Thank you," I said when she'd finished.

She smiled. "What about something to drink? Tea, coffee?"

We settled for tea, all of us, and sat numbly without saying much. I watched the boys sipping and shook my head and trembled a little. What if one of them had died?

At one of the other tables sat the Kahns and near them Gladys Golman and her sister, Tillie Harmel, who was in great pain. Karl Kahn had ordered a coffee and brandy but when it came and he tried to drink it he found he was shaking so badly he couldn't get the cup to his mouth. It rattled against the saucer as he set it back on the table. Renate, watching him, called over a doctor.

The doctor looked briefly at Karl and led him through to a small room close by the tea lounge and examined him. His blood pressure had gone racing up and the doctor immediately gave him two shots of Valium. Karl relaxed and in a while felt calmer, got up and walked back to Renate at the table. His coffee had gone cold in the cup.

We heard a voice say over the public address system that the airport was closed until further notice. *Closed.* It seemed odd that we had closed an entire airport.

Taj Gulam came up with his clipboard.

I took the pen to write our names and addresses, the pen shaking a little on the paper. It didn't look like my writing.

"How are you all," he asked the boys. "Feeling better?"

They just stared at him blankly and didn't say anything.

"I want to go to the toilet," Garett whispered. I looked at the others and we all needed to go.

"I'll take Garett and you look after Brendon," I suggested to Lynn and off we went, each holding one by the hand.

It took Garett and myself a while to find the place, wandering about the building, the people still watching us with those peculiar horrified expressions. We spotted the door and went in.

It was a multipurpose room; in one corner stood a barber's chair and next to it a Kenyan barber in a white outfit who greeted us. There was another man with a mop and a bucket and we were halfway across the room before we realized he had been washing the floor. It was still wet and we had walked over it in our muddy shoes.

"I'm so sorry," I apologized. "We've just come from the air crash and I didn't think."

They both looked startled.

"You have been in the jumbo jet?" the barber asked, his eyes big.

"Yes, we managed to get out before it blew up."

The barber whistled, shaking his head. "You have been in that thing! *Hei*, you are lucky people!" He came over and shook our hands and after him, the man with the bucket.

"Please," the barber said, "take off your shoes. We will clean your shoes."

"No, we can do it," I objected.

But he wouldn't stand for that. "We will do it," he insisted. "Come, give them to me."

We took off our shoes, handed them over and went through to the toilets. We heard them talking, the voices echoing off the tiled walls, while we were in there. We washed and dried our faces and when we came out saw they were wiping the last of the mud from the shoes with paper towels.

"It's very kind of you." I took the shoes and put them back on my feet and helped Garett with his. "I'm sorry I don't have any money. We lost everything."

The barber smiled and shook his head. "What happened?" he asked. "Why?"

"It came down," I said. "There wasn't enough power, I think the engines cut out, and we came down and hit the road. The jumbo broke in half and caught on fire. We were just lucky. We were in the front half."

The barber made another whistling noise through his teeth and clasped my hand between both of his. "God is with you," he said. He did the same to Garett and we both shook hands again with the cleaning man.

"Please, you must enjoy yourself now in Kenya," the barber said when we got to the door.

"Thanks very much," I said, feeling touched by it all.

Back in the cafeteria we found a busload of survivors had

arrived, some wounded, some in torn clothing, who were being treated by the medical team. At the table Lynn reminded me, "Pat and Ian will be waiting for us in Johannesburg and they'll be worried to death when they hear about the crash. Can't we phone them or something?"

"But they'll be at the airport."

"There must be someone we can phone. What about your mother? What about my mother?"

I looked out the door and saw a group of newsmen staring in, cameras slung from shoulders, notebooks in their hands. Before leaving South Africa for Europe I had worked for the *Pretoria News* and the newspaper group had a correspondent in Nairobi. If I could find him perhaps I'd be able to get a message back home.

"I'll see what I can do."

I went over and asked the newsmen if they had seen Henry Reuter, if he was around somewhere. No, they said, shaking heads, and started to ask me questions: "What happened?" and "How did you get out?" and "Did you know it was going to crash?" and "how did it feel?" and so on, and so on. I told them how it was, but I wasn't thinking clearly, and I was anxious to find Henry Reuter. I must have sounded really muddled. An airline official came out of the cafeteria, pulled me back into the room and told the newsmen to leave us alone.

"I'm trying to find a friend of mine," I said angrily, sitting down again at our table. I looked across at Lynn. "What's the matter with these people?"

She shook her head.

I went back to the doorway to the reporters still grouped around. There were television cameramen with them now. A man in a gray suit came toward me, introduced himself, shook hands, and said: "I believe you're looking for Henry Reuter?"

"Yes, is he here?"

"He's in Ethiopia. Something's brewing up there and I've been asked to substitute for him."

"Oh, good," I said, pleased. 'I'll give you a story if you do me a favor. I want you to telex the *Pretoria News* and ask them to tell my family we've all survived."

"Certainly."

He wrote down the details and I started to tell our story — again.

Tom Scott spent about an hour wandering, dazed, around the airport building. At first he headed for the tea lounge, then changed his mind and decided he needed to visit the toilet. He headed back the other way, stopping to ask people: "Excuse me, do you know where the bathroom is?" They pointed out the way and he set off, but when he got there he didn't feel like going to the toilet anymore. He turned around and started back to the cafeteria. At the cafeteria he decided he really had to go to the toilet. Off he went down the passageways, asking people for directions. He couldn't make up his mind what he wanted to do, so he continued wandering around the building.

When he finally returned to the cafeteria a British Airways stewardess handed him a cup of coffee. Holding onto something seemed to help and he sat down with some of the other crew members, sipped slowly at the steaming cup and tried to puzzle his behavior out. Later he would realize it had all been due to shock.

John and Jean Bing and Terry Partridge rolled up outside the airport building in a Land-Rover driven by one of the Italian construction workers from the Sogene site. They arrived in the cafeteria at the same time as Captain Krack and sat near him and the rest of the crew. Captain Krack was deeply distressed and sat with his face in his hands, muttering and shaking his head. He kept looking up and asking, "Why?"

His surviving crew members stared blankly at him. Some of them shrugged and one patted the captain's back, trying to calm him, but he would not be pacified.

I went up to him, not realizing how he was, put a hand on his shoulder and said: "I thought you did damned well getting that plane down."

Captain Krack swung round. "You call that bloody mess out there good?"

I stepped back, surprised.

"Well — " I mumbled, shrugged, thought, forget it, and walked away.

Then everyone started to get up from the table, some limping and being helped along, all of us stringing along in a line behind Taj Gulam and the other officials as they led us through the door.

"Where are we going?" someone asked.

"To the restaurant," a voice said behind us. "Someone said they're going to give us a meal."

Lynn looked at me. "I don't feel like eating anything."

"Neither do I."

But we walked on in that peculiar procession of shocked, mud-stained, bloody and ragged people and found ourselves being led through the back corridors of the airport. We went up stairs, along past closed doors, as if we were walking in a maze. It seemed a terribly complicated way of getting to the restaurant and we couldn't understand why they took us that way. They might have been trying to keep us away from the newsmen and television cameras down in the departure concourse, but no one told us and we kept on walking.

Once we came to a wet stretch of floor and there was a man on his knees next to a bucket. He looked up, startled, and we halted. The officials up ahead spoke to each other, opened a door and led us a different way past the wet floor. Eventually we came out in a restaurant and were invited to sit down.

The officials began to discuss something with the restaurant staff and I guessed we would not have a meal there after all. Perhaps there were too many of us?

Taj Gulam was carrying his list of survivors from group to group. He had forgotten to list nationalities. I wrote down ours and he carried it away.

When he returned he announced that there would not be a meal after all. "We will take you to the Hilton and you can eat something there," he told us, adding, "Please follow me." The survivors filed out of the restaurant, heading onto a sunny balcony behind Taj Gulam and the officials, and walked down a flight of stairs to the ground floor. We joined in behind Mother Dietlinde, came out through a side entrance into a carpark and there stood a bus. We climbed aboard and found seats together.

When all the survivors were aboard the bus started, turned around in the carpark and nosed out onto the tarmac road, maybe a little too quickly. I thought, "Too fast! He'll kill all of us!"

The others were white-faced and tense, their hands gripping the seats. We were terrified of anything that moved.

The bus slowed and stopped at the Mombasa–Nairobi highway. There was traffic speeding from left to right in front of us and I thought, "Oh God, no, I can't take much more of this." I tried not to look.

The bus began to swing out, turning right into the highway that led to the city, and a woman's anguished voice cried out from the back: "Please drive slowly! *Please!*"

One Seat Apart

THE DOCTORS AND STAFF at Nairobi Hospital were having a hectic day. It had all started out so normally, but at 8.03 A.M. a chilling message was telephoned through to the head nurse: "A jumbo jet has crashed. Prepare for a major disaster."

The woman left what she was doing and hurried through to casualty. An orthopedic surgeon had just arrived and took the hospital's emergency "crash box" and, together with the casualty nurse, raced off to the scene of the wreck. They were followed by the hospital's almoner, who was also a trained nurse, and a casualty officer.

They reached the site at 8.35 A.M., about forty minutes after *Hessen* had crashed, and surveyed the devastation. By that time the firemen had gotten the fire under control, but the wreckage was still burning, still shooting clouds of smoke into the air. Most of the seriously injured survivors had left the area and were, even as the hospital team stood there, being rushed to Nairobi by ambulance. A few shaken people wandered about near the road and the hospital team went forward to see how they could help.

Back at Nairobi Hospital the off-duty casualty nurse had been called in and the School of Nursing was quickly converted into a receiving area for lightly injured survivors. The students who had been at lectures were brought in and the hospital's consultants and general practitioners in the city were telephoned and asked to come and help as soon as possible.

Nairobi had never had a major air disaster. No one knew quite what to expect. They guessed that the small casualty department with its six couches would probably be overwhelmed by the numbers of injured. They had no idea how many there would be, but they thought apprehensively of the size of the 747s and knew the jets could carry hundreds of passengers.

Dr. Gerd Kampf-Emden, the injured managing director from the first class cabin, was one of the first to arrive. His ambulance came screaming up, stopped outside casualty and he was helped in, still wearing his blood-soaked Lufthansa slippers.

He was impressed by the organization of the hospital. The casualty staff took him directly to a couch, eased off his slippers and socks, cleaned him up, gave him a pain-killing injection and stitched the two-inch gash in his foot. They dressed the wound and checked him for any other damage and discharged him.

Outside, a car gave him a lift to the West German Embassy. As it began to move off he saw ambulances drawing up outside casualty and numbers of people being helped out, some on stretchers.

Among this group was Hans Offerbroich who had severe multiple fractures. He was having difficulty breathing and arrived in a critical condition. The hospital staff rushed him through to intensive care. Some of the others who arrived with him had serious neck and spinal injuries and were cut and bruised. For a while the X-ray department was crowded as radiographers and nursing staff battled to assess all the injuries. More survivors arrived as they worked.

Dropped off outside the hospital by a Land-Rover, Malcolm Solts limped in, his legs bleeding and bruised. He stayed about four hours at the hospital while staff examined his throbbing right knee and checked him over. They told him he had torn a ligament.

Solts waited around while the more seriously injured were rushed through. The reception area looked chaotic and disorganized. There were injured people everywhere and he saw members of the cabin crew sobbing uncontrollably nearby. Someone was screaming and demanding immediate attention but mostly the people seemed to be sitting or standing about looking dazed and shaken, as if they couldn't believe this was really happening.

There was no way of contacting family or anyone at all — the telephones were tied up. And no one seemed to know where they should go after they had been treated. Later Lufthansa officials arrived and ferried those who had been discharged down to the Hilton Hotel, gave them money for clothes and essentials and helped to arrange telephone calls, but for a long time up at the hospital, survivors sat around feeling bewildered and abandoned.

The ambulance carrying Carol Mall and Margaret Hooker came racing through the city, siren screaming. The early morning traffic pulled over to let it through as it headed for the Kenyatta National Hospital. It was the only ambulance to arrive there; all the others went directly to Nairobi Hospital.

Carol Mall was unconscious, critically injured with a broken neck. She was carried into the hospital for emergency treatment. The doctors examining her found she was paralyzed in all four limbs and had what looked like friction burns on her back, probably the result of being pulled from the burning aircraft. She also had a broken ankle, a broken thumb and cuts on her face. Hospital staff hovered about her all day as her body fought against massive shock and severe injuries. The next day she would be transferred to the intensive care unit at Nairobi Hospital and treated there for weeks before being flown out on a stretcher, heavily sedated, to the United States.

Several times in the weeks and months ahead her life would hang in the balance through complications caused by her injuries: she would develop a stress ulcer and hemorrhage so severely that she would need sixteen pints of blood in one day and doctors would have to perform emergency surgery, and weeks later, back in Washington D.C., she would develop pneumonia with near cardiac arrest and would spend six weeks in an intensive care unit. After a year and a half in hospitals and nursing homes her condition would stabilize, but she never returned to normal life.

Carol Mall and Margaret Hooker had sat side by side only one seat apart, not guessing what a tragic difference that would make to their lives. Margaret staggered away from the wreckage badly wounded in the foot and arm, dragging her companion with her, but Carol never walked again. Her paralysis was permanent — she would need care and attention for the rest of her life.

One seat apart. The roles could so easily have been reversed. And Margaret Hooker shook her head in sad bewilderment as a doctor neatly stitched her wounds. A shot killed the pain but she felt dazed, almost anesthetized by the horror of what she had been through. Strangely, she had bled very little and guessed this was because she had been covered in jet fuel. Later, infection would set in, delaying the healing process.

When Margaret's wounds were dressed and bandaged, she was driven down tree-lined streets to Nairobi Hospital to spend the night. She thought, if nothing had happened we would probably have been landing in Johannesburg about now.

The orthopedic surgeon who had returned from the wreck with the emergency team quickly joined the casualty team. He had a busy morning. Nearly all the seriously wounded had fractures and needed orthopedic treatment. The surgeon noted a high incidence of spinal injuries. Five passengers and two crew members had fractures or strains of the lower back — a result of sitting strapped in, head dropped down between the knees in the crash position while the jet went hurtling into the earth faster than an express train. Six others were brought in with "whiplash" injuries to the neck and three people had both neck and back strain.

By mid-afternoon fifty-five survivors had been treated, including one passenger who had no injuries but was treated for shock, and eight crew members. Twenty-three had been admitted.

Among those needing attention was Flight Engineer Rudi Hahn who had his dislocated shoulder reduced. Copilot Schacke was treated for cuts on the head. Five of the crew were admitted.

One thing that surprised and puzzled the hospital staff: none of the people they treated had been burned.

Newsmen wandered through the wards looking for survivors who would talk to them. In St. George's Ward they found Captain Heinz Peper who had been sitting in the rear of *Hessen*. He was the only survivor from the tail compartment. Of all the escapes that day, his was perhaps the most miraculous.

"I could see from the very start of the takeoff run that something was wrong," he told reporters. "By the time we were halfway down the runway it was clear to me that we were traveling too slowly."

He had sat staring out, watching the runway blurring past, and it had seemed to him as if the jet had only lifted at the very end of the runway. The jumbo then began to shudder.

"I knew this was it," the young captain said quietly. "I lowered my head between my legs in the emergency position and waited for the crash. Seconds later we were shaken by the first impact.

"I can't remember exactly what happened then except that the seats and passengers in front of me disappeared into a big crack at my feet. My section of the plane was thrown sideways and I lost consciousness."

His eyes far away, he paused, thinking. "I don't know how long I was blacked out, but when I woke up, I saw a huge hole in the fuselage next to where I was sitting. I undid my seat belt and fell head-first out of the crack."

He landed in a field of fire, the grass around him burning fiercely. He struggled to his feet and blacked out again. When he recovered consciousness he scrambled to his feet and ran for his life.

"I had not gone twenty-five meters before a huge explosion knocked me flat," Captain Peper remembered. The blast wrecked the compartment he had been sitting in, hurling flaming wreckage across the bush. The explosion and fire killed all those he had been sitting with a few moments before. But here he was, alive, shaken yet still able to talk coherently to his amazed companions.

There were touching scenes in the streets of Nairobi. Following an appeal broadcast by the Voice of Kenya radio station hundreds of people gathered outside the city's blood donor center to give blood for the injured survivors. They stood several hours in the sun, people of all races, black, white and brown, appalled by the tragedy that had occurred in the fields outside their city.

Simeon Njenga, the officer in charge of the center, spoke movingly of their reaction. "The response has been wonderful," he told newsmen. "They are anxious to save the lives of their brothers and sisters."

People donated 528 pints of blood that day, but in the end the hospitals' own blood banks supplied all that was needed.

Waiting for News

IN BRITAIN THEY heard the news before breakfast. At 7 A.M. BBC radio newscasters reported that there appeared to be no survivors in the world's first jumbo jet disaster at Nairobi, East Africa.

Among the millions listening was the secretary of Sheffield sales engineer Terry Partridge. She realized with a shock that her boss was on that plane. He had been booked for an economy return flight from Manchester via Frankfurt to Johannesburg for a two-week sales trip to South Africa to seek orders for his firm's heat-resistant materials.

She telephoned Terry's boss and the two of them, numbed by the news, discussed what they should do. What *did* one do at a time like this? It was too early to telephone Terry's wife; she would probably not be awake yet. They decided to wait and to send someone round to the house at nine o'clock, by which time there would probably be more news. They hung up, listening fearfully for the next newscast. When it came, they heard there were now estimated to be fifty survivors.

Jill Partridge had just gotten back from taking her six-year-old daughter Sarah to school and was starting the household chores at home in Worrall, a town near Sheffield, when some people arrived at the door. It was Terry's business colleague Colin Atson and his wife, Vera.

"Come in," she told them cheerfully. She thought, Vera's probably not feeling too well and has come to spend the day with me.

Once inside the Atsons asked Jill to sit down and said they had something to tell her. She looked at them and sat down, suddenly anxious.

"The plane that Terry was on has crashed . . ."

She heard what they said but could not believe it.

". . . it was only half full and about half the people have survived. So there's a good chance that he's all right."

Jill sat numbed, horrified by the vision of Terry in a crashing plane. Her first thought was, I'm sure he's all right. He must be all right. It was a desperate, illogical thought, but she felt quite sure that he was alive.

There was little anyone could do but wait for more news and Jill sat there, comforted by the Atsons, and doing her best to reassure her three-year-old daughter Helen who seemed to know that her mother was upset.

Jill telephoned her sister eventually and they talked about telling their parents but again they decided that it would be better to wait until they heard something definite. Jill put the phone down, wanting to keep the line clear for any news.

The minutes dragged by. Ten, twenty, thirty, forty minutes — all that time her mind was in a whirl and she repeated to herself, I'm sure, so sure he's all right.

At that moment, thousands of miles away in Nairobi, Terry Partridge was stepping off the bus that had brought survivors in from the airport. He walked into the lobby of the Hilton Hotel and went directly to the reception desk.

"I want to send a telex message to England," he said. "I've just been in the jumbo crash."

It was arranged in minutes.

The telephone rang in Sheffield. Colin Atson stepped over and picked it up. The office had just received a telex message from

Nairobi: Terry Partridge was alive and unhurt and checked in at the Nairobi Hilton.

Jill Partridge burst into tears; young Helen cried too. Jill held her daughter to her, sobbing with relief after the most wonderful telephone call of her life.

In Johannesburg news of the disaster spread and shocked families began an agonizing wait for news of their loved ones. Mrs. Gisela Hutton was at home, dressed and ready to leave for Jan Smuts Airport when she heard. She and her husband were leaving to meet her eighty-eight-year-old father, Erich Hesse, who was flying in for a few weeks' holiday.

When her husband arrived he looked shattered. He had telephoned the airport to check the arrival time of the Lufthansa flight and had been told there would be a delay "of uncertain duration." Worried, he telephoned his friend, the editor of the Johannesburg *Star*, and was told the jet had gone down over Nairobi.

Others heard while they were waiting at the airport. Mrs. Anna Eybers screamed and collapsed on the concourse. Her daughter Petro and son-in-law Manfred Fischer were aboard that flight, returning home to their children Werner, seven, and Helane, five, at the end of a working holiday in Germany.

Later, when she had recovered from her initial shock, she went home with her grandchildren. The children tried to cheer her up, telling her their mother and father would return eventually. Listening to them almost broke her heart.

That afternoon she heard that both Petro and Manfred had survived and told journalists, "November the twentieth is the most wonderful day I can remember."

Later, as more details became available, her daughter's name was removed from the list of survivors, but Manfred Fischer was said to be alive and at the Hilton. Despairing and confused, Anna could only wait, praying that it was all due to bureaucratic muddle; that when the official list of survivors was issued the names of Petro and Manfred would be on it.

"Petro didn't want to go on vacation to Germany," she told a reporter while she waited. "At the last minute she asked me if I wanted to go in her place. She wasn't even interested in packing her suitcase and only finished when I helped her."

Mrs. Eybers would wait through the night. In the morning officials told her both Petro and Manfred were dead.

The morning would also bring heartbreak for electronics engineer Mr. P. Fitz who had been waiting for hours at Jan Smuts Airport for a reunion with his wife Heide-Marie and his children, one-year-old Nicole and Bonnie, aged four. Fitz had been transferred to Johannesburg for three years by the West German Siemens company and had come on ahead to make arrangements for the family. He had been in Johannesburg only two weeks.

At the Holy Childhood Convent in Eshowe, Zululand, the days of waiting were almost over. The mother superior was coming back from home leave in Germany.

The convent children were jumping up and down with excitement, as Sisters Edith, Elkana and Martina climbed in the Volkswagen Combi that would fetch Mother Dietlinde from the airport in Durban. The engine sparked into life, the sisters waved and the van went slowly down the dusty road.

The three sisters stopped off to buy school exercise books for the next year, later calling at the Mari Stelle Mission to pick up Sisters Liboria and Theodelind who had decided to travel with them to greet Mother Dietlinde. The five women reached the airport at about 12.30 P.M. and heard a voice announce over the public address system that the connecting flight from Johannesburg had been delayed fifty minutes.

Back at the convent in Eshowe a telephone call came through from Germany. It was Mother Ehrengarda speaking from Würzburg-Oberzell where Mother Dietlinde had spent her home leave.

The jumbo jet carrying Mother Dietlinde, she told a horrified sister, had crashed over Nairobi. The news had just been flashed on German radio and television. No one knew if anyone had survived.

The news spread quickly through the convent and the school. Children burst into tears and the sisters called an immediate midday break. Everyone went into the church to pray.

At Durban airport the delayed aircraft from Johannesburg finally landed at 1.50 P.M. and the sisters watched eagerly for that familiar figure. Fifteen passengers got off but Mother Dietlinde was not among them.

They were on their way over to the information desk to ask what had happened when they saw the mother superior from Mari Stelle and another sister approaching. Telephoned by the nuns of Eshowe, the mother superior had decided to drive out to the airport herself with the dreadful news. Now, grim-faced, she told them, "Mother Dietlinde's plane has crashed at Nairobi."

Officials at the information desk suggested to the shocked and bewildered nuns that they drive to the Lufthansa office in Durban for more news. They arrived in time to hear that it was now known that ninety-one people had survived the crash. Twenty-one were receiving treatment in the Nairobi Hospital and the others had been booked in at the Hilton Hotel.

The airline's list of survivors had only forty-five names on it.

Was there a Geis among them?

The officials checked. Yes, there was a Geis. A Mr. Geis.

The sisters could only wait — hoping there had been a mistake — that Mr. Geis was really Mother Dietlinde Geis.

After three hours of waiting, the telephone rang again at the Holy Childhood Convent in Zululand. It was Mother Ehrengarda calling from Germany.

"Mother Dietlinde is among the survivors!" she said.

Sister Urbana clutched her skirts and went running off toward the school.

The children and sisters in the school heard her excited shouts coming nearer.

"The mother is alive!"

At midnight in Johannesburg, Beryl Laburn was waiting

anxiously for news of her husband, Bob. An airline official working through the night telephoned to give final confirmation that Bob Laburn was not on the survivors' list. It should be presumed that he was dead.

The news came as a shattering blow to her and her family. Until then they had held out hope that in the confusion Bob Laburn's name had been overlooked, and would eventually appear.

Repeated telephone calls throughout the day to Lufthansa's Johannesburg office and to the Rand Water Board where Bob worked had told them nothing. Bob Laburn was not among the survivors, nor was he among the dead who had been identified. It was possible that he was one of the charred corpses awaiting identification in the Nairobi City Mortuary, or that his body was still hidden in the burned-out wreckage at Embakasi.

In her anguish, Beryl Laburn clung to one last hope. Someone, she knew, had tried to telephone her that day at her office but had failed to get through. This small unexplained event gave her something to cling to in those dark hours of the early morning.

As morning broke, the flag on the Rand Water Board building overlooking the Library Gardens in Johannesburg was lowered to half mast as a mark of respect to the chief engineer.

Soon after nine o'clock, a telegram arrived and was taken in to the Board's secretary. It stated that Bob Laburn had back injuries but was reasonably well and in the Misericordiae Hospital in Nairobi. There was a telephone number.

The secretary didn't know what to think. The telegram had been sent at about 11 A.M. the previous day. Should he accept this, or should he accept Lufthansa's much later news that Bob Laburn was dead?

He decided to try the telephone number.

The call puzzled the sisters at the Misericordiae Hospital, but they did what the caller asked. They went through and asked their patient to tell them the names of his wife and children.

Bob Laburn, lying in bed, was indignant. What did the hospital want personal information like that for? And then he became apprehensive: perhaps something had happened at home. He gave them the information, wondering what it was all about.

Back in Johannesburg the secretary let out a shout: "Bob's alive! It's all bccn a mistake!"

Bob Laburn's colleagues let out a cheer and a short while later the flag was pulled up to the top of the mast.

It was 10 A.M. when Beryl Laburn heard the news, and wept with relief and joy.

Bob Laburn's name had been on the survivors' list all along, the family discovered later, misspelled. There was no such person as "Mr. L. A. V. Bern" but on that morning no one was complaining. Bob Laburn had come back from the dead.

Survivors

AT THE HILTON HOTEL, survivors crowded around the telephones in the lobby, struggling to put through international calls to relatives and friends.

It felt strange to be there. We had prepared ourselves for an arrival in Johannesburg, but instead we wandered about feeling lost. I kept thinking there was something I should be doing, but I couldn't guess what it was.

Lynn was holding her back and wanted to keep walking. It hurt to stand still and I kept urging her to see a doctor.

The boys clung to us, their vivid red pullovers making them stand out, and people came over to touch them and fondle their hair. They seemed unusually quiet and bright-eyed.

We were a strange group of people in our torn, bloodstained clothes, some of us bandaged, some missing shoes. The porters stared at us. There was nothing for them to do; none of us had any luggage.

A telephone call brought Jock and Betty Leslie-Melville to the Hilton, and it was an emotional meeting. They had spent hours trying to find out what had happened to us and now here we were, shaken but virtually untouched.

In our room overlooking the city, the sun shining brightly on the buildings, we tried to relax. Betty went off to buy us new toothbrushes and a facecloth, and that gave us another shock — we didn't even own a toothbrush! All we had were the clothes we were wearing. It was like being born again.

Elsewhere in the hotel Malcolm Solts, back from treatment at the hospital, had managed to get through to his wife Andrea in Boston. She hadn't even heard about the crash. The call came through at 6.15 in the morning and woke her up.

Tom Scott had been out and bought himself a new toothbrush, razor, and shaving cream and then, because there was nothing else to do, he went swimming in the Hilton pool. He lay in the sun and thought how odd it all was; life simply going on as usual after what had happened that morning when he had come close to dying. Now he lay basking in the sun, filled with feelings he couldn't express.

Tom was in deep shock although he didn't realize it. Two mornings later he suffered a massive attack of trembling and couldn't keep down any food. By the afternoon he felt like he was losing consciousness, a strange tingling went through his body and he lost control of his actions. He was terrified but eventually the shaking stopped and never came back.

It was lunchtime. Lynn had gone off to the hospital to have her back checked and I went down to the ground floor restaurant with the two boys.

"You can have anything you like," I told them, "because today's such a special day."

"Anything?" Garett asked.

"Whatever you like. You choose."

"Even ice cream?"

"Even ice cream."

They ordered two huge plates from the waiter and I watched them spooning it up, making it last, and thought how lucky we were to be able to sit here and eat.

I was struggling over something more substantial, finding it difficult to eat, and looked up as someone came through the door. I stared hard, not really believing my eyes. It was the old man who had been sitting behind us in *Hessen*, a bloody dressing now on his forehead. The man I had thought was dead. He couldn't possibly have gotten out in time, but here he was.

I got up and shook his hand.

"Am I pleased to see you!"

He showed me his attaché case and took out his passport. I read his name: Erich Hesse.

"We thought you were dead."

He smiled and shook his head. He spoke only German, but he understood. He had survived.

Evening fell over Nairobi, the orange of the sunset fading swiftly from the horizon. Hermann Hennecke was speaking on the telephone to his wife and children in Johannesburg.

"I'm fine," he was telling them. "And I'll be home as soon as I can get a plane out of here."

"Do we have to go to school in the morning?" asked seven-year-old Ralf, and he heard his father chuckling at the other end of the line.

In a restaurant in a different part of the Hilton, the ten surviving American members of the Unitours safari group were meeting to decide whether to continue their trip or return home.

They sat in a room hung with African spears and shields and zebra skins, wearing the same clothes they had crashed in, and talked quietly. They all wanted to go on with the tour. There didn't seem to be any sense in heading home; they were already in Africa, but they sadly missed the smiling face of their guide Maya Galitzine, and the companionship of the Solibakkes.

An orchestra gathered to play for the evening's dancing and the smell of steaks frying over charcoal wafted through. Cooks in white hats bent over the sizzling food as music began to play.

Elinor Senkler suddenly remembered the special dinner she and Edmund had planned to have in Johannesburg tonight. Twenty-six years ago today —

"Eddie," she reminded him, "it's our anniversary!"

There were congratulations from the group.

"We must celebrate!" someone called out.

Soon champagne corks were popping and the Senklers were being toasted. Smiling waiters carried in trays of lobsters caught in the Indian Ocean and the evening took on a festive air. There were interruptions: newsmen visited the table for interviews and from time to time members of the group were called away to answer long-distance calls from the United States.

On it went into the night. Listening to the music and the voices around her, Elinor Senkler thought, this is more than an anniversary. We're really celebrating today's miracle — the miracle that we're alive.

Several floors above the restaurant I lay with Lynn in the half-dark of our hotel room, trying to sleep. The telephone had kept ringing, once from a journalist in Melbourne, several times from newsmen in London. The *Argus* newspaper group in South Africa phoned to ask me to cable an exclusive survivor's account in the morning.

We lay there, feeling exhausted, but unable to sleep. We could see Garett and Brendon through the connecting door of the next room sleeping on their beds, two dark little heads of hair against the white of the pillows.

There was a cry. Garett jumped up from the bed shouting: "Get out! Get out!"

He started to run wildly around the room, climbing over the furniture.

Shaken, we ran through.

We caught him at the door, tugging desperately at the handle, sobbing, "We've got to get out! Get out!"

Lynn cuddled him. "It's all right, darling. You're only dreaming."

As he tried to fight free I saw his face. He was terrified, his eyes glazed, and it was as if we were not there. We took him back to bed, stroking his forehead, talking gently, and after a long time it seemed he had drifted off to sleep.

We went back to our bed and lay down, watching him through the doorway.

"Did you see his eyes?" Lynn asked. "He couldn't see us. Do you think he's all right?"

"I don't know."

A while later it happened again. The rush to the door, the shouts, the tears. We quietened him again, but we couldn't sleep after that, waiting for the next time.

I lay on my bed and wondered, my God, what has that crash done to him? What does a thing like that do to six- and seven-year-olds?

The lights still glowed in the Nairobi City Mortuary as officials worked on, trying to identify the fifty-nine shrouded bodies spaced out on the floor. Many had been disfigured by fire and the only clues to their identity came from charred passports, watches and jewelry which had been labeled, numbered and stored in plastic bags.

Most of the victims died on impact, the pathologists decided: flung out or fatally injured as they sat strapped in their seats. They presumed that in most cases death had come from other injuries before burning. Nine people had died from smoke asphyxiation and seven had severe injuries which would have prevented them from escaping.

Another eleven died from burning and nine of these had been trapped in the aircraft by severe injuries unable to move. Their bodies were found in the forward half of the aircraft, among the burned-out remains of the economy class "quiet" section and the first class compartment.

The mortuary team worked on grimly while the first relatives were winging their way in through the night sky.

The next day a nonscheduled Lufthansa Boeing 707 was taxiing out for takeoff carrying a group of survivors returning to Germany. Among them was Dr. Gerd Kampf-Emden, his foot heavily bandaged.

There was total silence as the jet rumbled out and turned in the stopway. The passengers looked pale and nervous. It must have taken a lot of courage to fly again twenty-four hours after the crash, Dr. Kampf-Emden thought, mentally detaching himself for a moment from the group.

And then the takeoff roll started.

No one spoke. Hands tightened across stomachs, clasped armrests. The plane hurtled faster and faster down the runway. Some people instinctively bowed their heads.

The nose lifted, the 707 hung there for seconds, and rose steadily up into the morning air. Passengers sat with eyes closed remembering what had happened the day before.

Minutes later when the plane had leveled off, thousands of feet up, the nose aimed for Frankfurt and home. Stewardesses came down the aisles carrying trays of champagne and soon the survivors were swapping tales with each other and the cabin crew. Laughing and relaxed, they flew on.

Dr. Kampf-Emden looked down at his glass brimming with light-headed bubbles. They had all faced death together; there was a bond between them that would remain after the champagne had gone and the flight was over. It was wonderful to be alive and going home, but underlying it all, he felt a bitter sadness. He couldn't forget those whose lives had ended back in the fields of Nairobi.

Aftermath

WITHIN A MATTER OF days most of the survivors had flown out of Nairobi. A few, like us, stayed on at the Hilton Hotel, deeply shocked, bewildered and confused. In a way, it seemed enough simply to have survived. Why make decisions? We could so easily have been dead.

But we could only put off making decisions for so long. Soon, apart from critically injured Hans Offerbroich and Carol Mall, we were the only survivors left in Nairobi and airline officials wanted to know what our plans were.

We were in a peculiar situation. We had tried to get our tickets changed so we could get off the flight in Nairobi but had failed. After accepting the fact that we would arrive in Johannesburg instead, quite suddenly we ended up where we had wanted to be — Nairobi.

But now, everywhere we went in Nairobi we were reminded of the horror. Walking down a street in the shopping district we would find ourselves, and especially the children, the center of attention.

"Excuse me," someone would say, "but weren't you in the jumbo crash?"

"Yes," we would say.

"We recognized you from the children —"

And then the questions would start. Soon a large crowd would gather on the sidewalk and the only way we could escape was by telling our story. It happened again and again, and each time the story was told, we relived the terror.

Another factor that made our situation unique was the children. At six and seven, they were the youngest survivors. They were also probably the most disturbed.

They relived the crash in the most horrifying nightmares and would wake up screaming and shouting, sometimes sobbing bitterly. Garett would leap up from his bed and run about the room panic-stricken, as if he were trying to escape, his dreams so vivid and his reactions so terrifying that for a time we thought he was losing his mind.

There was terror even in daylight. Sudden bangs or explosions, or an aircraft swooping low overhead, would cause them to burst into tears and clutch desperately at us. It seemed sometimes as if their whole personalities had changed. They had become clinging, insecure and easily frightened children. They could not sleep with the light off — interestingly a phenomenon often encountered in war-shocked or injured soldiers. This state of affairs lasted for more than a year. Both were afraid of all forms of transportation and, given the choice, preferred simply to stay where they were and not go anywhere.

Shocked ourselves, we found it difficult to give them the psychological and physical comfort they needed. Then, one morning, an express letter arrived from my sister-in-law Pat in Johannesburg, South Africa. "Please won't you all come *home*! It's so terrible not being able to see you," she wrote, and in our highly distressed condition we had no defense against such a plea. We read the letter with tears in our eyes and decided that we had to go south, right away from Nairobi and its memories of death and flaming destruction. We needed to be with the rest of our family in a place we knew.

But none of us could bear the thought of flying. We were afraid we would crack under the strain. Perhaps we could go by ship? We approached Lufthansa's passenger service manager Taj Gulam and by noon the next day it was all fixed up: the airline would pay for our train journey to the port of Mombasa, and the sea voyage between Mombasa and Durban, South Africa.

Ten days after the crash that had changed everything, a diesel locomotive pulled our train slowly out of Nairobi and headed east for the Indian Ocean. Night had fallen and in the dark we clicked steadily past the aircrash site on the far side of the Mombasa road. A great bank of red landing lights gleamed brightly near the end of the airport runway, and beyond that there was darkness, nothing to see. But we knew what lay there and stared silently out into the African night until the last of the airport lights had slid from view. Life's journey had ended in that field for fifty-nine fellow travelers; ours continued, winding its way on into the unknown. It was a strange and deeply moving moment.

The journey was not pleasant. We were woken with a jolt the next morning and heard the diesel's horn sounding in alarm. Our adrenalin coursed wildly. It turned out that two giraffes had stepped in front of the train and had been killed. The impact damaged the locomotive so we sat back to wait for a replacement steam engine from the next station, wondering nervously how good the traffic control was on East African Railways. The engine took two hours to arrive and we spent the time watching far-off buck through the haze, sitting in the heart of the Tsavo National Park. It would have been paradise for tourists, but we were too shaken up to appreciate it and half-expected another train to plow into the back of us. We eventually made Mombasa three and a half hours late, but luckily the S.S. *Karanja* was still moored at the quayside and we sailed that evening.

A few days later we struck a storm in the Mozambique Channel. The small ship rolled and shuddered. Spray pounded over the deck outside our cabin and in the lounge some joker remarked: "This ship is doomed!"

It was the worst thing anyone could have said. Our nerves were near breaking point. Despite tranquilizers, we couldn't sleep and spent a terrifying night listening to the creaking of the ship, feeling each sickening rise and fall.

But we made Durban, steaming into harbor on a bright December morning and there, waving from the top of the ocean terminal, were Pat and Ian. We had come full circle; they had seen us off from Jan Smuts Airport in Johannesburg nearly three months before and now they were the first to welcome us back.

As we stepped onto dry land, I vowed never to travel anywhere again, but I knew that would be impossible, especially as I was a journalist.

Ten months later, a U.S.-based newspaper asked me to fly to Nairobi to write a series of articles on the UN environment program in Nairobi. I agreed. Could I really do it? I wasn't sure, and went through hell in the weeks before the flight. I had terrifying nightmares: 747s nose-diving into the earth, or falling back tail-first on takeoff, exploding in a fireball of flame.

The impending flight also had a bad effect on my family. It didn't help to explain the law of averages to the children; they had been in an aircraft and it had crashed. They had sleepless nights, nightmares and tears; I seriously considered not going. It wasn't fair to put them through all this agony.

But in the end I went ahead. Before I knew it, one October evening I was climbing the steps below the huge hunched shape of a Lufthansa Boeing 747 — destination Nairobi. Superstitious to the last, I had asked for the same seat I'd had on the doomed *Hessen*, but the best they could do was two rows ahead. No matter, I was still between the wings, the strongest section of the jet.

I was desperately reading the safety instruction sheet when the jet began to move. I felt a terrible panic and had a sudden sick feeling that the jet would explode in flames. We were all so vulnerable, just little bits of flesh and bone.

The jumbo taxied to the head of the runway and the captain announced we were ready for takeoff. My mouth went dry, I wiped the sweat from my face and sent up a prayer. The engine noise built up, the jet shook and we were off. So slow, it seemed.

There was a rushing, airy sound and the runway lights flashed by faster and faster. I had a cushion and blanket resting on my knees, and my legs were braced, pushing against the floor.

When the nose lifted, I felt so nervous I thought I would be sick. The wheels lifted — the critical moment — and I was sure we would crash back down. But we carried on climbing, the engines whining steadily through the night sky, the lights falling far below, specks in the night.

The 747 eventually leveled off, but I couldn't relax, and watched the clock all the way. I tried to read, but couldn't. Each patch of turbulence terrified me and I flew the whole way with the seat belt fastened. When we touched down smoothly in Nairobi at about midnight, I had made it, but I felt awful.

Later, when I began working on this book and spoke to other survivors, I discovered my experience was not unique. They had all suffered. Some shared similar long-term effects — insomnia, nightmares, extreme nervousness, claustrophobia, a lack of judgment relating to size and distance, and moods of deep depression.

Manfred Wengerek decided his office was too small when he returned after the crash and bought a huge factory. He and his staff moved in, but after a while he realized the building was ridiculously large, sold it and moved to smaller premises.

"I took a bit of a knock, lost a few thousand, but I had to get out of it," he said. "I don't understand what made me act that way."

Terry Partridge had a different, deeply traumatic experience. He had a sleepless night after the crash, but felt well enough the next morning to fly on to Johannesburg to continue his business assignment. The flight south was an anxious one, but he thought he had got through it reasonably well. Then, in Johannesburg, he began to feel shaky and the feeling worsened steadily. He went to see a doctor who prescribed a course of sedatives.

The next day he felt even worse and burst into tears while speaking to his wife Jill on the telephone. He decided to cut short his trip and fly back to Britain as soon as he could get on a plane.

Back home again, he was still deeply upset. Several mornings he woke up sobbing for no apparent reason and felt depressed. He went to see his doctor and, trying to explain what was wrong with him, broke down in his consulting room. It was, Terry Partridge recalled, one of the worst times he could remember.

His doctor prescribed a two-month course of strong sedatives and advised him not to travel for a while. The two months were hell. "My nerves were pretty shot and I couldn't really function or talk to anybody for any period of time without getting upset," he said later. "Anyway, I took the tablets and at the end of two months I seemed to be almost back to normal."

It was three months before he flew again and he took the same route he'd been on when he crashed: Manchester–Frankfurt–Nairobi–Johannesburg. The airline staff did their best to distract him and by the time he reached Frankfurt he'd had so much to drink he wasn't sure if he was on a plane or a bus.

He woke up in Nairobi with "the worst hangover I've ever had in my life," but the alcohol had anesthetized him to the fears of the journey and gotten him over that psychological hurdle.

Once, flying over South West Africa/Namibia, his plane passed through severe turbulence and he felt "very frightened indeed, my heart thumping like I've never experienced before."

Since then, he has flown many thousands of miles around the world and feels he has come to terms with his fears. As long as the flight is normal, he is not anxious, but finds himself "deeply affected" by anything unusual — flying through a storm, or being bounced about in turbulence.

Another who suffered was Gerd Kampf-Emden who had returned to Germany the day following the crash. Together with his wife, he flew again two months later, taking the the same route as the crash flight. The 747 landed safely in Nairobi, refueled, and then failed to restart. Time dragged, Gerd sat strapped into his seat, nerves on edge, waiting. What had gone wrong?

The pilot announced that takeoff would be delayed due to a defect in one of the engines. Repairs would take a while but the flight would be resumed shortly.

Dr. Kampf-Emden aproached the Lufthansa crew and explained that he had been in the *Hessen* crash and now felt extremely nervous about this flight. Would it be possible for him and his wife to transfer to another aircraft for the final leg of their journey to Johannesburg?

The airline staff were most understanding and within half an hour the Kampf-Emdens boarded the incoming British Airways flight and took off for Johannesburg. They arrived safely and heard later that the Lufthansa had flown in about three hours late after an uneventful flight.

In May 1975 came a new drama at Nairobi. Dr. Kampf-Emden was aboard a British Airways jumbo bound for Johannesburg. After refueling, the big jet thundered down the runway, the nose wheel lifted, and the jet rose sluggishly off the earth. Dr. Kampf-Emden felt an icy hand clutch at his heart. Something was going wrong again at Nairobi! The jumbo wasn't climbing normally. Like *Hessen* six months before it was flying parallel to the ground.

The pilot's voice broke in to inform passengers that he was having problems with one of the engines and would have to land.

Dr. Kampf-Emden sat nervously in his seat as the jet struggled to gain altitude. Then it turned back and lined up for the landing approach. The jet dropped gently and coasted in over the grassy outfield. There was a bump, the wheels touched, and there was the shudder of reverse thrust. The jumbo slowed and taxied back to the terminal building where Dr. Kampf-Emden stepped out of a defective plane for the third time in six months. He and his fellow passengers were put up in a hotel for the night.

Now, Kampf-Emden says grimly, his colleagues are superstitious. "Never fly with Kampf-Emden, you are sure to run into trouble!" they say.

Will he ever really recover from the trauma of the *Hessen* crash? He is not sure. "Even today, although I have flown often since then, I haven't got over the events of Nairobi," he reports. "I am extremely anxious during takeoff and landing because I know that these are the dangerous flight maneuvers. I react very nervously and do not sit calm and collected in airplanes like I did in the past."

In order to gain compensation for their suffering, twenty-nine survivors have brought a group action against the Boeing Company of Seattle, Washington, alleging that the company was negligent in the design, construction, production, manufacture, service, certification, testing, sale and inspection of *Hessen*. As a result, the group alleges, the aircraft was "in a defective and unsafe condition, and unsafe and unfit for sale and use in the way and manner for which it was properly intended." The group also claims that Boeing was "negligent in failing to warn of known defects" in the Boeing 747 aircraft. Boeing has denied all the allegations and is opposing the action.

The most seriously injured survivor, Carol Mall, did not join the action because of a private settlement with Boeing. Crippled for life by the crash, she was accompanied back to the United States by her sister, Henriett Smith, who is now Carol's companion and pays her bills, shops for her groceries, and makes her telephone calls.

In 1976 Carol bought a house in Sumter, South Carolina, and had it specially adapted to enable her to lead as independent a life as possible. She still needs nurses or nursing assistants to care for her but with the help of mechanical aids she is able to type and write short letters and has taken three courses at the local state university with her sister Henriett acting as her "attendant." In a recent course on American history Carol achieved an "A" and an exemption from the final examination — a remarkable accomplishment for a woman who has to record each lecture on tape and then laboriously reduce the recording to notes using her mechanical aids. Her health continues to be a problem but, according to her sister Henriett, "we do our best together and only live one day at a time."

Unlike those of us who suffered emotional and psychological shock, Carol Mall can never hope for complete recovery. Yet what happened to her could so easily have happened to any one of us; today we continue to lead our comparatively normal lives while hers has been ruined. It's a sobering thought and one the months and years have not been able to dull.

The scars of Nairobi run deep. Neither Lynn nor I can hear of another air disaster without experiencing a feeling of cold, wordless horror. It engulfs us like a wave of nausea, a sick hollow feeling that centers in the stomach and lasts for minutes. It's as if, for a few moments, we experience again the fear and anguish of crashing. We *know* what the crash victims have gone through, that it doesn't ever happen so quickly that you know nothing about it.

A few days before I traveled to London in 1979 to work on this book an American Airlines DC 10 dropped an engine on takeoff at Chicago, flipped slowly onto its back and plunged into the earth, killing all those aboard. Lynn and I were listening to the radio when the local station broadcast a recording of conversations in the Chicago control tower during those last few seconds. A voice yelled that a DC 10 had shed an engine. The tower called repeatedly to the crippled jet, would the pilot like to return? There was no response, only a crackling on the radiowaves.

Desperately the tower called again and again, and then a voice cried out, "Oh, my God!"

We saw it then in our minds, a huge explosion, a dark cloud shooting skyward. All those people dying. For a few moments neither of us could speak, then Lynn said: "They knew. They knew all the time."

And that, I think, is the real horror of an aircrash — speeding to your death, strapped in, knowing what is happening but being unable to do anything about it. The feeling of utter helplessness, of being in the grip of forces totally beyond human control is the impression that hangs most vividly in the minds of Lynn and our two sons because it was their last experience of flying; they have not flown since the crash. For them it is a vicious circle: they will not fly because they are afraid; but they will not come to terms with their fears until they do fly again.

Is there a way out of this dilemma? I thought that time might solve it for the children, that eventually they would be mature enough to rationalize it for themselves, but so far this has not happened.

In the early days after the crash the children played bizarre games, building toy planes with Lego blocks and hurling them down the stairs to see how many plasticine "passengers" survived. They also burned paper planes. We looked on this as a form of therapy, an acting out of their fears.

Despite this, mention of flying sends both Garett and Brendon into a highly nervous state. Of the two, Garett appears to be the most deeply affected, probably because he was fully awake throughout the terrifying ordeal, while young Brendon was asleep and actually had to be woken after the impact.

We have assured Garett that we will not force him to fly, that he can always travel by ship wherever we go as a family, but with the world caught up in an energy crisis, most of the major shipping lines are cutting back on their passenger services. The few passenger ships still sailing are far more expensive than planes and they don't always sail the routes we might want to travel. So, until the advent of the new energy-efficient sailing ships, it seems as if flying will be our only option. But, short of heavily sedating them, how do you get terrified young air-crash survivors to fly again?

Recovery is a long and gradual process and no one can say if it is ever complete. I like to think my own recovery started back in the lobby of the Nairobi Hilton Hotel the day of the crash when I first heard the story of the three drunk Germans.

They had been on holiday in Kenya, so the story goes, and were catching the Lufthansa flight to Johannesburg. A group of friends went to see them off and joined in a last-minute "celebration" to round off the wild party they'd had the night before.

By the time the jet arrived from Frankfurt the three young tourists were all but staggering. Led onto the aircraft by airline staff, they strapped each other in; the jet raced down the runway, lifted off and crashed. Somehow the three men managed to find their way to an emergency exit and tumbled out of the burning jumbo. They ran blindly through the bush back to the airport terminal, sat down at a table and shouted for drinks and their luggage.

They were still shouting when the first of the injured survivors arrived and were taken into a side room for first-aid treatment. Annoyed by the noise from the next room, a nurse eventually went up to the three Germans and told them, "Please keep your voices down. These people have been in a frightful air crash and you're upsetting them."

Extremely confused and heavily intoxicated, the young men had difficulty in understanding the woman, let alone talking quietly. All they could think of was getting their luggage and another round of drinks. It was only later that someone realized that they too had been in the crash and were in deep shock.

I heard this story from several different people but, despite extensive inquiries, was unable to authenticate it or identify the three Germans. I mention it because it is an amusing tale and gave many survivors their first real laugh.

There is another strange story and this one is true.

In one of our suitcases I had placed a number of unpublished newspaper articles and short stories, including one titled *In the Shadow of Kilimanjaro* that I kept in a used envelope originally addressed to Friends of the Earth in Pretoria, South Africa. The story was set in Nairobi and was based on an idea I thought of during my first visit in March 1974. It was still incomplete, but had a dramatic opening, with the main character landing at Nairobi after a long and nervous flight from San Francisco. How poetic, I thought, that the story should have been burned up in a crash at the same airport!

Unknown to me, Lufthansa investigators found the envelope containing the story among the wreckage, thought it was a piece of damaged mail and sent it on to the Friends of the Earth address in Pretoria. Friends there received it, read it, guessed it belonged to me, popped it in a large envelope and mailed it to me in Johannesburg many weeks later with instructions that I should finish the tale — they wanted to read the ending.

I finished the story, but I fear magazine editors think it too bizarre — I've been unable to sell it. But I do still have the small brown envelope that the story traveled in. Stamped on the outside in purple ink are the words, "Retrieved from air crash on 20 November 1974 at Nairobi."

The smell of the air-crash still clings to that envelope and if I close my eyes and sniff deeply it all comes back in a rush: burning kerosene and billowing smoke, wreckage strewn across the bush, fleeing, horrified survivors. And I feel deeply moved — and grateful that, like my short story, the four of us went through hell . . . and survived.

What Happened and Why

INVESTIGATIONS BEGAN WITHIN hours of the accident and were conducted by the East African Community Accident Investigation Branch, assisted by two members of the United Kingdom Accidents Investigation Branch. Also participating were representatives of the states of registry and manufacture, and of the Boeing company and Lufthansa German Airlines.

Evidence was gathered from a variety of sources. The crash site was examined; the distribution of wreckage was plotted in order to reconstruct the crash sequence. The flight recorder was recovered intact and the investigators also had access to tapes from the control tower. Boeing ran tests on the wing flaps, the pneumatic system and its related warning lights. Finally, the cockpit crew were interviewed.

Lufthansa conducted an internal inquiry of its own and later dismissed the Commander, Captain Christian Krack, and Flight Engineer Rudi Hahn. The copilot, First Officer Hans-Joachim Schacke, was reduced in rank.

Supported by *Vereinigung Cockpit*, the West German pilots' association, Krack and Hahn instituted a legal action against the airline for unlawful dismissal. Krack had, in the meantime, obtained a suspension from flying on medical grounds which safeguarded his pension. The legal action was eventually ended by a compromise settlement.

The East African Community report was officially released in Nairobi in July 1976. A summary described the accident:

The aircraft was operating Lufthansa flight 540/19, a scheduled international passenger and cargo service from Frankfurt, Germany, to Johannesburg, South Africa, with an intermediate stop at Nairobi. During the takeoff from Nairobi the crew felt vibration or buffeting after liftoff and suspected engine trouble. Subsequently the Commander, suspecting wheel imbalance, raised the landing gear.

The copilot, who was handling the aircraft, noticed a complete lack of acceleration and had to lower the nose in an attempt to maintain airspeed.

The aircraft lost altitude and the rear fuselage made contact with the ground approximately 1120 metres beyond the departure end of runway 24. Parts of the aircraft struck an elevated road 114 metres further on and it started to break up.

The main portion skidded an additional 340 metres during which time it turned to the left through approximately 180 degrees. The aircraft was destroyed by impact and subsequent fire.

The report reached the following conclusions:

FINDINGS

1. The crew were properly licensed and experienced.
2. The aircraft had been maintained in accordance with an approved maintenance schedule and its Certificate of Airworthiness was valid.
3. The weight of the aircraft and its centre of gravity were within the prescribed limits.
4. The aircraft took off with the leading edge flaps in the retracted position, with the result that it became airborne in a high drag, partially stalled condition.

5. The loss of ground effect during the climb-out together with the probable presence of slight adverse wind sheer and the opening of the landing gear doors during the retraction cycle contributed to a further reduction in performance with the result that the aircraft descended and struck the ground.

6. Following the introduction of a modified procedure which involved the closing of the pneumatic system bleed valves, the revision of the cockpit checklist after starting was completed did include a requirement for checking the re-opening of the bleed air valve switches, but did not specifically call for a check on the pneumatic system.

7. After the engines had been started the flight engineer omitted to open the bleed valves, thereby rendering inoperative the pneumatic system which powered the leading edge flap units.

8. The indications of leading edge flap position prior to takeoff could not be positively established. However, it is extremely unlikely that the flight engineer's annunciator panel indicated that all the leading edge flap units were in the correct takeoff position.

9. In view of the inherent possibilities of incorrect leading edge flap operation and the critical nature of leading edge position during the takeoff phase, adequate warning of incorrect position should have been provided. The existing indication system in use at the time of the accident did not meet this requirement.

10. Cockpit procedures did not call for any cross checking by the commander of items on the flight engineer's panel.

11. The accident could probably have been averted had the pitch angle been reduced and power been increased sufficiently early in the flight.

12. The pilots did not take effective recovery action in the short time available to them because they did not identify the semistalled condition of the aircraft until alerted by the stall warning system shortly before the aircraft struck the ground.

13. The stall warning system did not give adequate warning of the critical condition of the aircraft because it was not programmed to take account of leading edge flap position. Had it been so programmed, its operation at liftoff might have alerted the crew in time to affect a recovery.

14. This accident was preventable. Inadequacies in international incident reporting procedures and effective follow-up action could be considered a contributory factor.

CAUSE

The accident was caused by the crew initiating a takeoff with the leading edge flaps retracted, because the pneumatic system which operates them had not been switched on. This resulted in the aircraft becoming airborne in a partially stalled condition which the pilots were unable to identify in the short time available to them for recovery.

Major contributory factors were:
1. The lack of warning of a critical condition of leading edge flap position.
2. The failure of the crew to satisfactorily complete their checklist items.

RECOMMENDATIONS

It is recommended that:
1. The takeoff configuration aural warning system programme on Boeing 747 aircraft should be modified to include leading edge flap position.
2. The takeoff configuration aural warning system on Boeing 747 aircraft should be excluded from the list of allowable deficiencies.
3. Consideration should be given to the incorporation of leading edge flap position in the aircraft's stall warning programme.
4. Consideration be given to the inclusion of a pneumatic duct low pressure warning on the Pilot's Annunciator Panel.
5. Consideration be given to amending operating procedures where necessary to include a cross-check by the Commander of important items on the flight engineer's panel.
6. In Boeing 747 and similar aircraft, States of Registry should require the carriage of a multi-channel flight data recorder compatible with ARINC 573 or equivalent characteristic.
7. In Boeing 747 and similar aircraft, consideration should be given by States of Registry to require the installation and use of hot microphone cockpit voice recorder circuits during the takeoff, approach and landing phases.
8. Implementation of adequate international incident reporting procedures, as initiated in the Accident/Incident Reporting System (ADREP) of the International Civil Aviation Organisation, including effective follow-up action, should be enforced.

ACTION

The Chief Inspector of Accidents in East Africa took immediate action to alert world airlines as soon as it became apparent that the leading edge flaps had failed to extend prior to *Hessen*'s takeoff on November 20.

On November 23, 1974, three days after the crash, following a request from him and the United States National Transportation Safety Board, the Federal Aviation Administration (FAA) recommended an interim flap inspection procedure. All Boeing 747 operators were urged to insure that the flaps were extended to the normal takeoff position before leaving the ramp and to get a qualified ground observer to make a visual check.

On December 6, 1974, the manufacturer telexed all Boeing 747 operators, briefly describing the circumstances of the Nairobi accident and emphasizing the necessity for checks on bleed valve switches, leading edge circuit breakers and alternate system switches.

On December 11, 1974, the FAA issued a Notice Of Proposed Rule Making proposing an Airworthiness Directive which would require modifications to the existing leading edge flap indication system, and the addition of an input from the leading edge flap logic unit to the takeoff aural warning system.

On December 16, 1974, Boeing suggested alternative modification proposals:

a. that the amber light on the pilot's panel would illuminate if any one leading edge flap unit was not fully extended and the trailing edge flaps were at a takeoff setting

b. that the limit switches in the leading edge flap motors would cause inputs to the takeoff aural warning system if any flap unit was not fully extended and the trailing edge flaps were at a takeoff setting.

The FAA accepted these proposals and issued an Airworthiness Directive covering the modifications, effective from March 24, 1975. The directive was to be complied with within five months.

COMPENSATION

Survivors who had lost clothing and luggage were compensated, in excess of the international agreement, by Lufthansa within a few weeks. Several survivors who had been injured and relatives of those who were killed claimed damages from the airline's insurers. In many cases, settlements have been negotiated.

List of Victims

Abbott, Alan, 41
Assmann, Horst, 35
Assmann, Leone, 35
Assmann, Renate, 3
Behrmann, Boy, 69
Birth, Klara, 44
Braue, Günther, 39
Braue, Gustav, 76
Brodersen, Horst, 32
Broutschek, Hildegard, 61
De Candia, Francesco, 35
Eckert, Anette, 2
Eckert, Helga, 32
Fickenwirth, Karin, 34
Fickenwirth, Werner, 34
Fischer, Manfred, 34
Fischer, Petro, 27
Fitz, Bonnie, 4
Fitz, Heide-Marie, 33
Fitz, Nicole, 1
Frankenberg, Helmut, 44
Friedrichs, Harry, 63
Gabusi, Marco, 25
Galitzine, Marie (Maya), 44
Grant, Anthony
Hämmerle, Elisabeth
  (Sister Bona), 72
Haug, Gerhard, 47
Hohenleitener, Hilaria
  (Sister Blandina), 52
Isebeck, Dr. Klaus, 38
Jäger, Lothar, 40
Kriegleder, Renate
  (Stewardess), 24

Lauricks, Sibille, 37
Lockyer, Victor, 37
Maier, Theresia
  (Sister Annuntiata), 63
Malmquist, Lars, 29
Merrick, John (Paddy), 52
Nachtsheim, Helge
  (Mickey Mouse stewardess),
  35
Nachtsheim, Klaus, 39
Nemitz, Joachim, 29
Nietser, Rolf (Steward), 28
Panayotou, Stilianos, 24
Pantazopoulos, Ioannis, 48
Rönnfeldt, Reiner, 24
Schmidtsdorff, Dr. Peter, 36
Schönhöfer, Resi, 69
Schwarzenberger, Martin, 32
Seegers, Wilhelm, 60
Seidel, Ernst, 58
Selbach, Rita (Stewardess), 22
Setzer, Anna (Sister Richardis),
  62
Skogberg, Kaj, 46
Smits, Hubert, 62
Solibakke, Alfred, 77
Solibakke, Veronica, 77
Stosch, Elke, 30
Teufel, Siegfried, 31
Vidal, Traude-Liese, 44
Vohs, Manfred (Steward), 27
Zahn, Peter, 35

Index